How to use this book

Targeting Writing Skills **is a comprehensive program for teaching students the fundamentals of grammar and the basic structure of the three main types of texts: Informative, Imaginative and Persuasive.**

This book is organised into four terms, each consisting of eight units of work followed by a review. The first unit of each term focuses on grammar, primarily on the structure of sentences. The following six units are organised in pairs, with each pair focusing on a different text type. The first unit of each pair introduces and explains the structure and features of the text type using an annotated example text. The second unit provides students with a stimulus appropriate to the text type and prompts to write their own text using the model as a guide.

Each term follows the same order:

- Informative texts — Units 2 &3, 10 & 11, 18 &19, 26 & 27
- Imaginative texts — Units 4 & 5, 12 & 13, 20 & 21, 28 & 29
- Persuasive texts — Units 6 & 7, 14 & 15, 22 & 23, 30 & 31

The final unit in each term provides students with additional practice in writing either an imaginative or persuasive text by innovating on an existing text to change characters, setting, text type or point of view. As these are the two main text types that students encounter in NAPLAN assessments, the additional practice helps prepare them for the tests.

A review of work that has been covered concludes the term.

While the units are organised into terms, it is not necessary to complete them sequentially. Teachers may choose units from any section of the book that suits their teaching needs. However, it is recommended that the grammar units be completed in order as each one builds upon the previous one.

The writing topics in this book were selected for their relevance to the Australian Curriculum V9, including HASS, Science, General Capabilities and Cross-curriculum Priorities so that these books can be used for lessons in writing across the curriculum.

The units are presented using a gradual release of responsibility model:

1. Information is presented and explained in a detailed model.
2. Students are supported to identify features of the model.
3. Students use the model as a guide to write a text of their own about a given stimulus.

Prior to writing their own texts, students are reminded of the required structure and parts of speech that they need to incorporate. They plan, draft and receive feedback on their text before writing a revised draft. At the conclusion, they conduct a self-evaluation to determine how well they adhered to the structure and included appropriate parts of speech.

Australian Curriculum Correlations

Code	Description	Pages
English: Language		
AC9E5LA02	understand how to move beyond making bare assertions by taking account of differing ideas or opinions and authoritative sources	34, 48–51, 66–71
AC9E5LA03	describe how spoken, written and multimodal texts use language features and are typically organised into characteristic stages and phases, depending on purposes in texts	4–19, 22–37, 40–55, 58–73
AC9E5LA04	understand how texts can be made cohesive by using the starting point of a sentence or paragraph to give prominence to the message and to guide the reader through the text	4–19, 22–37, 40–55, 58–73
AC9E5LA05	understand that the structure of a complex sentence includes a main clause and at least one dependent clause, and understand how writers can use this structure for effect	38–39, 56–57
AC9E5LA06	understand how noun groups can be expanded in a variety of ways to provide a fuller description of a person, place, thing or idea	3, 21, 26
AC9E5LA08	understand how vocabulary is used to express greater precision of meaning, including through the use of specialist and technical terms, and explore the history of words	4–7, 22–25, 40–43
AC9E5LA09	use commas to indicate prepositional phrases, and apostrophes where there is multiple possession	21, 26
English: Literature		
AC9E5LE01	identify aspects of literary texts that represent details or information about historical, social and cultural contexts in literature by First Nations Australian, and wide-ranging Australian and world authors	8–11, 16–17
AC9E5LE03	recognise that the point of view in a literary text influences how readers interpret and respond to events and characters	8–11, 12–15, 52–53
AC9E5LE04	examine the effects of imagery, including simile, metaphor and personification, and sound devices in narratives, poetry and songs	16, 26–29, 62–65
English: Literacy		
AC9E5LY03	explain characteristic features used in imaginative, informative and persuasive texts to meet the purpose of the text	4–19, 22–37, 40–55, 58–73
AC9E5LY06	plan, create, edit and publish written and multimodal texts whose purposes may be imaginative, informative and persuasive, developing ideas using visual features, text structure appropriate to the topic and purpose, text connectives, expanded noun groups, specialist and technical vocabulary, and punctuation including dialogue punctuation	4–19, 22–37, 40–55, 58–73

TARGETING WRITING SKILLS YR 5 © PASCAL PRESS ISBN 9781925726282

Contents

Contents

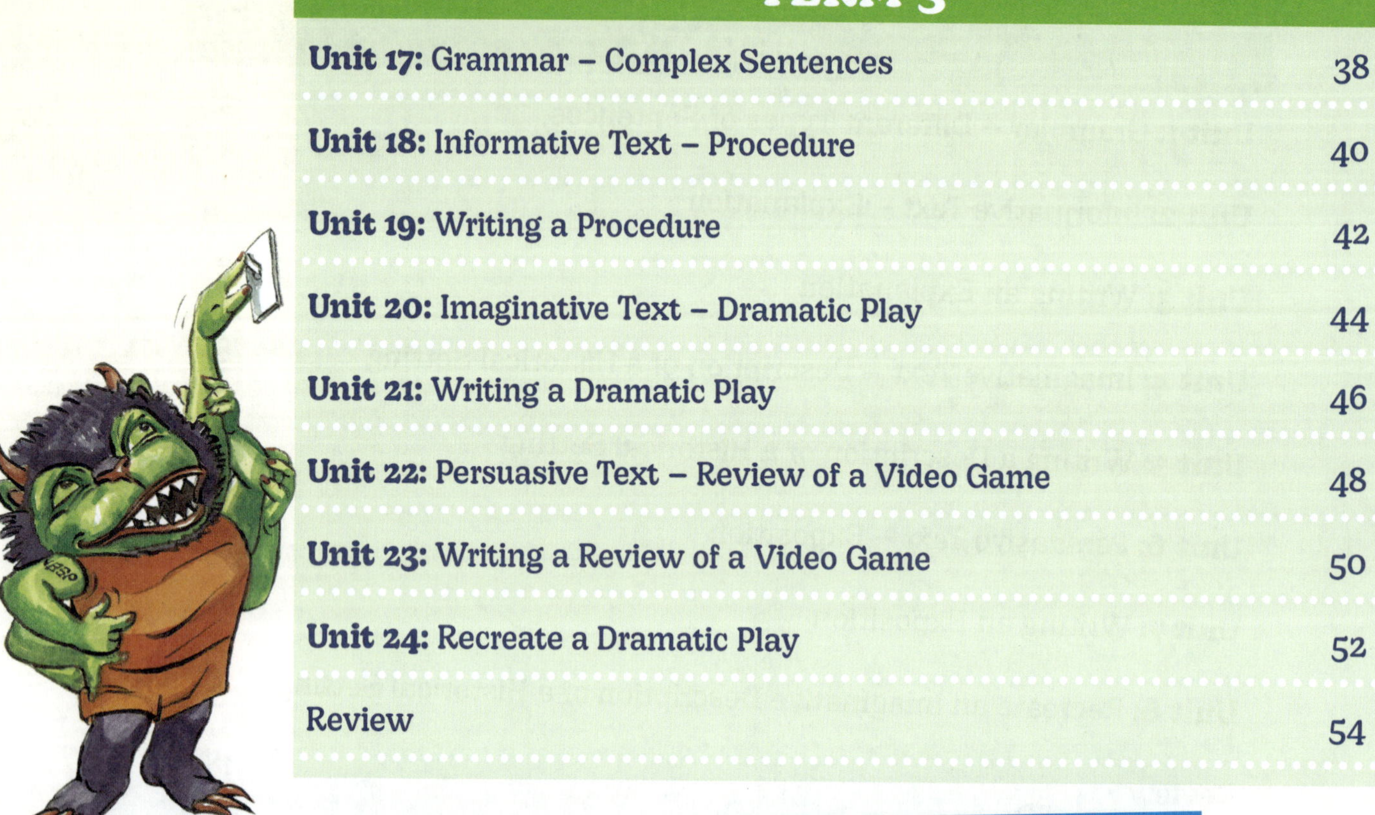

TERM 3

TERM 4

TARGETING WRITING SKILLS YR 5 © PASCAL PRESS ISBN 9781925726282

Australian Curriculum Correlations

Code	Description	Pages
Science: Biological sciences		
AC9S5U01	examine how particular structural features and behaviours of living things enable their survival in specific habitats	22–25
Science: Physical sciences		
AC9S5U03	identify sources of light, recognise that light travels in a straight path and describe how shadows are formed and light can be reflected and refracted	4–7, 18, 40–43
HASS: History		
AC9HS5K01	the economic, political and social causes of the establishment of British colonies in Australia after 1800	8–11, 16–17, 57
AC9HS5K02	the impact of the development of British colonies in Australia on the lives of First Nations Australians, the colonists and convicts, and on the natural environment	8–11, 16–17, 58–59
AC9HS5K03	the role of a significant individual or group, including First Nations Australians and those who migrated to Australia, in the development of events in an Australian colony	58–59, 72
HASS: Civics and citizenship		
AC9HS5K06	the key values and features of Australia's democracy, including elections, and the roles and responsibilities of elected representatives	66–71
HASS: Economics and business		
AC9HS5K08	types of resources, including natural, human and capital, and how they satisfy needs and wants	12–13, 19, 30–35

TERM ONE

UNIT 1

GRAMMAR Writing Sentences

A sentence is a group of words that makes sense on its own. It always has a verb. It usually has a subject and often has an object.

A **statement** is a sentence that gives information or an opinion. It begins with a capital letter and usually ends with a full stop.
Examples: *The first fully synthetic plastic was invented in 1907. (information)*
Plastic is the worst invention ever made. (opinion)

A **question** is a sentence that asks for more information. It begins with a capital letter and ends with a question mark. Questions often begin with who, what, where, when, why, how.
Example: *When was plastic invented?*
Questions may begin with other words too.
Example: *Did you know that plastic was invented over a hundred years ago?*

A **command** is a sentence that gives instructions or directions. It begins with a capital letter and may end with a full stop or an exclamation mark. The first word is usually a verb, and the subject (you) is understood.
Examples: *Stop using single-use plastic.*
Close the door!

An **exclamation** expresses sudden surprise, joy or fright. An exclamation begins with a capital letter and ends with an exclamation mark. Some exclamations are just one word. They may not have a verb and may not be a complete sentence.
Examples: *Wow! That's amazing! I knew you could do it! Yikes!*

1 **Read these sentences. Write S if the sentence is a statement, Q if it asks a question and C if the sentence gives an instruction/command. Write E if it is an exclamation.**

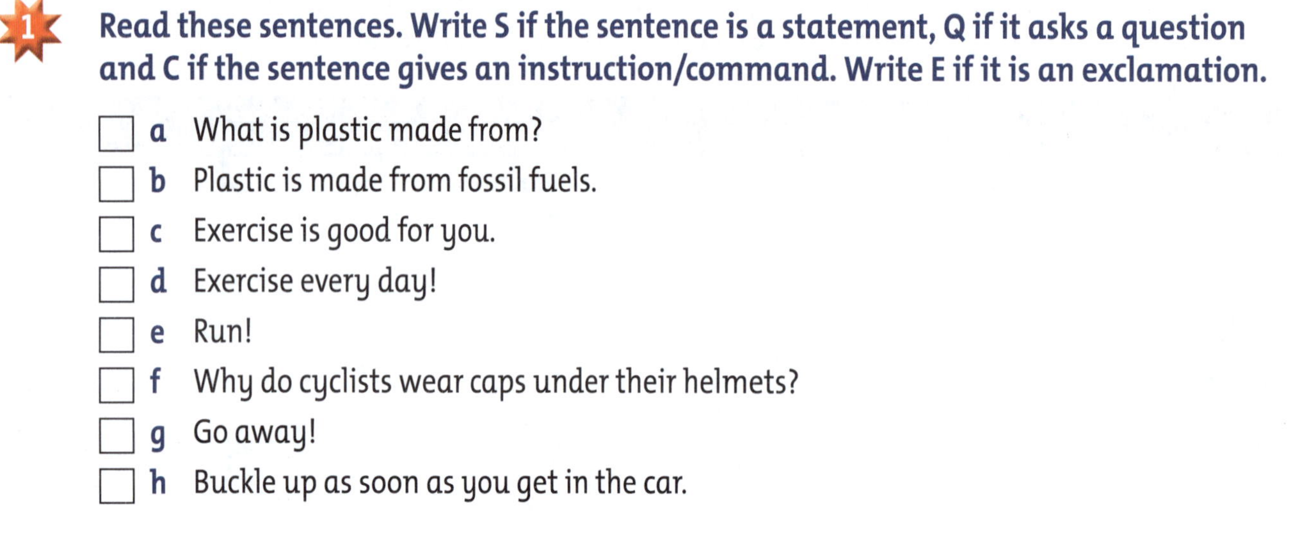

☐ **a** What is plastic made from?
☐ **b** Plastic is made from fossil fuels.
☐ **c** Exercise is good for you.
☐ **d** Exercise every day!
☐ **e** Run!
☐ **f** Why do cyclists wear caps under their helmets?
☐ **g** Go away!
☐ **h** Buckle up as soon as you get in the car.

2 **Look at this picture. Write some sentences of your own about the picture. Remember to punctuate your sentences correctly.**

a (S) ______________________________

____

b (Q) ______________________________

____

c (C) ______________________________

____

d (E) ______________________________

____

TARGETING WRITING SKILLS YR 5 © PASCAL PRESS ISBN 9781925726282

GRAMMAR Writing Sentences

The beginning of a sentence lets you know what type of sentence it will be.
Questions often begin with who, what, where, when, why, how. **Commands** usually begin with a verb. All sentences begin with a capital letter, but the punctuation we use at the end of the sentence depends on its type.

Read these sentences. Punctuate them correctly.

a did you go to the skate park on the weekend

b the shopping mall was closed due to the floods

c why did you do that

d hooray

This text has not been punctuated. Write it on the lines below with the correct punctuation.

stop why are you here you are not allowed in here didn't you see the sign the sign says no one must enter leave now

Sentences can be made more interesting and give more information by **expanding noun groups** using adjectives. Adjectives are words that describe or give more information about nouns.

Example: *I like apples.*
Expand: *I like crunchy, red apples.*

Example: *The girl won the race.*
Expand: *The youngest girl in the class won the cross-country race.*

Expand these sentences with noun groups to make the sentences more interesting.

a The dog chased the boy.

b The girl caught a fish.

c The gardener trimmed the hedge.

d The customer bought a cake.

When a lot of short sentences follow each other, the text may not flow, and the meaning may become disjointed.

Example: *My dog is Ziggy. He is black and white. He is a Border Collie. He likes to chew on shoes. He likes to chew on leather shoes.*

We can revise the sentences to flow more fluently by combining some of the adjectives to form noun groups.

Example: *My dog Ziggy is a black and white Border Collie. He likes to chew on leather shoes.*

Revise these sentences so that the text flows more fluently.

I live on a farm. It is an apple farm. It is just outside Stanthorpe. We grow Red Gala apples. They are juicy. They are delicious.

INFORMATIVE TEXTS Explanation

The purpose of an explanation is to explain how or why something in the world happens or how things work.

Purpose: This text explains how bicycle reflectors work.

Audience: The intended audience of this explanation is students who are learning about light and people who wish to have a better understanding of how bicycle reflectors work.

Context: Texts like this would be found in science textbooks and magazines, bicycle manuals and online.

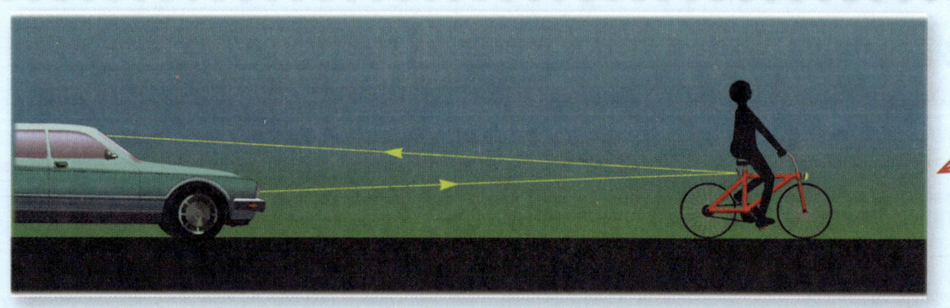

Explanations often include photographs or diagrams.

A title identifies the topic. It is often written as a question.

How Do Bicycle Reflectors Work?

Most bicycles have reflectors at the back, at the front and on the wheels. The purpose of the reflectors is to help keep the cyclists safe when riding at night. The reflectors warn other road users that the cyclist is there. But how do they work?

A series of paragraphs explains the process and the cause-and-effect relationships.

When light hits an object, it can go through it (transmit), bounce off (reflect) or be stopped (absorbed). A bicycle reflector is made to reflect light straight back to the light source.

Reflectors are usually made from transparent plastic. The outside surface is very smooth. This allows light (such as from a car's headlights or from a torch) to enter the reflector.

The back of the reflector is made up of lots of angled prisms. When the light enters the reflector, it hits the prisms. The prisms reflect the light back out in the direction it came from.

A concluding statement completes the explanation and links back to the introductory statement.

When the person who is close to the light source, such as the driver of a vehicle, sees the reflected light, they know that the cyclist is there.

Parts of Speech

Topic-related nouns, noun groups and technical language
- bicycles
- reflectors
- bicycle reflector
- light source
- transparent plastic
- angled prisms

Present tense
- have
- is
- warn
- hits
- are

Words to signal cause/effect
- purpose
- when

Adverbial phrases
- at the back
- at the front
- on the wheels
- when riding at night
- to the light source

 TARGETING WRITING SKILLS YR 5 © PASCAL PRESS ISBN 9781925726282

Structure of an explanation

Title
The title of an explanation identifies the topic. It is often written in the form of a question. Readers know that this explanation will explain how bicycle reflectors work.

1 Circle the title of the explanation.

Introductory statement
A general statement introduces the topic to focus the reader on what will be explained.

2 Highlight the introductory statement that introduces the topic.

A series of paragraphs
A series of paragraphs explains the process. Each paragraph has one main idea.

3 Highlight the main idea in each paragraph. In just a few words, list the main ideas below.

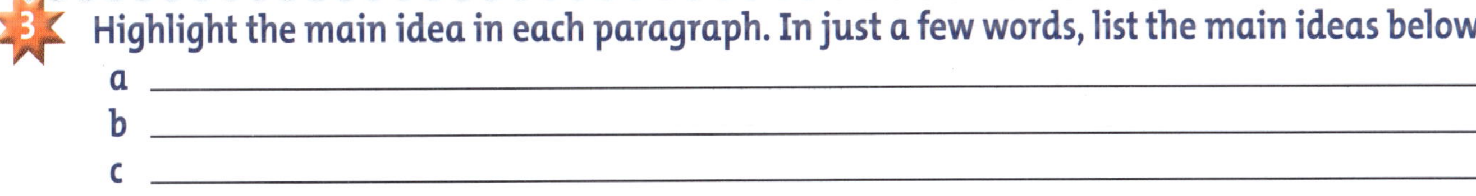

a ______________________________

b ______________________________

c ______________________________

d ______________________________

Language features of an explanation

Topic nouns
Nouns are the names of things in our world such as people, places, animals and things.
In an explanation, the nouns relate to the topic. They are **topic nouns**. Topic nouns are often repeated to link the text and ensure it can be understood. For example, *reflector* (singular) and *reflectors* (plural) are repeated throughout the text.

4 Circle each time the words *reflector* and *reflectors* appear in the text.

Subject
Sometimes *reflector* or *reflectors* is the subject of the sentence. The subject in a sentence *is* something or it *does* something.
Examples: *A bicycle reflector is made to reflect light.* (singular)
Reflectors are usually made from transparent plastic. (plural)

Subject–verb agreement
The verb must always agree in number with the subject. A singular subject needs a singular verb. A plural subject needs a plural verb.

5 Write the correct verb to complete these sentences.

a Reflectors __________ to keep cyclists safe. (help/helps)

b Motorists __________ the reflected light. (see/sees)

c Light __________ the prisms. (hit/hits)

Technical words
Technical nouns are specific to the topic and may need to be explained. In this explanation, *transmit, reflect and absorbed* are placed in brackets because more general terms are used in the text.

6 In your own words, write sentences to explain each of the terms.

a transmit ______________________________

b reflect ______________________________

c absorbed ______________________________

Writing an explanation

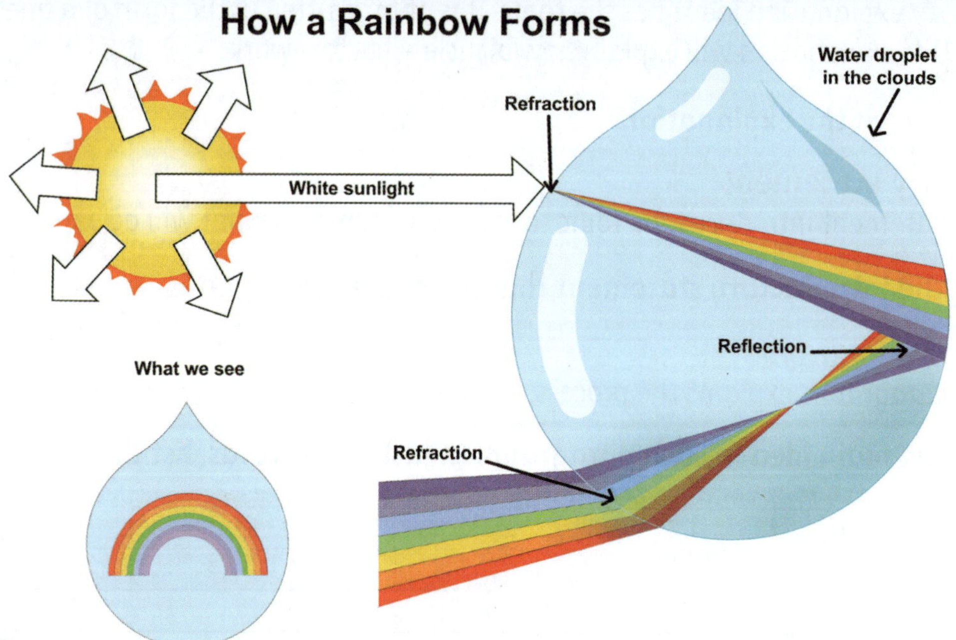

Plan

Use the following notes to write an explanation about how rainbows are formed.

Rainbows

- multicoloured arc in the sky
- made by refraction and reflection in certain conditions
- early morning or late afternoon when sun is low in sky
- sun must be behind you, water droplets in air in front of you
- sunlight must strike the water droplets at the right angle
- sunlight appears white – made up of all colours of the spectrum
- every colour has a different wavelength
- when light from the air enters a water droplet, it slows down and bends (refraction)
- reflects off the inside of the droplet – separates into different wavelengths (colours) – reflected at different angles
- speeds up and changes direction again when leaving the water droplet (refraction)
- we see the different colours of the rainbow: red, orange, yellow, green, blue, indigo and violet

 1 **Write the title for your explanation. Remember to write it as a question.**

____

 2 **Highlight the notes that you will use in a general statement to introduce your explanation.**

 3 **Use a different colour to highlight the notes you will use to conclude your explanation.**

 4 **Use different colours to underline the notes you will include in each paragraph. Each paragraph will include a different step of the process and include the cause and effect.**

5 **Write a few words to tell what each paragraph will explain.**

____

____

____

____

TARGETING WRITING SKILLS YR 5 © PASCAL PRESS ISBN 9781925726282

Draft

Now you are ready to write an explanation of how rainbows are formed.
Remember to:

- write your title as a question first
- write a general statement to introduce your topic
- explain the process in a series of paragraphs
- write a statement to conclude your explanation
- use present tense
- include explanations for any terms that may be difficult for readers to understand
- write in sentences with capital letters and full stops.

First draft

Write a draft of your explanation here.

Feedback

Ask your teacher, classmates or someone at home to suggest what you could do to improve your explanation.

Revised draft

Self-evaluation

I wrote ☐ the title as a question.
☐ an introductory statement.
☐ a concluding statement.
☐ in sentences with capital letters and full stops.
I used ☐ present tense verbs.

I explained ☐ the process in a series of paragraphs.
☐ any difficult-to-understand words.

IMAGINATIVE TEXTS Description of a historical setting

The purpose of an imaginative description is to describe or give details about a character, place or object.

Purpose: This text describes or gives details about the living conditions for convicts in a historical story set in the early days of Europeans living in Australia.

Audience: The intended audience of this imaginative description is children who enjoy reading adventure and historical stories.

Context: Descriptions like this would be found in novels and magazine stories. They do not usually occur on their own but form part of a longer text.

Descriptions may include illustrations.

A heading may be used to identify the setting.

Convict Life

Opening statements introduce the setting. The setting will be obvious by the words used and features described.

Ann and I entered the tent and Sergeant Scott got straight down to business.

"You have been assigned to look after my family and lodgings," he said. "As well as gathering water, preparing meals and cleaning, you will do anything my wife, Charlotte, requires of you. You will also assist with farming. Any questions?"

We shook our heads.

A series of sentences in one or more paragraphs describes the living conditions experienced in the setting.

At first, Ann and I lived in a small tent next to the sergeant's home while a hut was built.

Ann was in charge of cooking while I washed and mended clothes. I washed in a nearby stream and draped clothes over rocks and bushes to dry.

A statement concludes and evaluates the setting.

We knew how lucky we were to be working for the sergeant, rather than the harsh work of making bricks or building roads. All convicts worked — that was our punishment and why we were here.

Source: Adapted from *Banished*, Blake Education.

Parts of Speech

Topic-related nouns and noun groups
- tent
- sergeant
- lodgings
- farming
- harsh work
- convicts
- punishment

Adjectives
- small
- nearby
- harsh

Past tense
- entered
- got
- shook
- knew

Action verbs
- entered
- washed
- draped
- worked

First person narrator pronouns
- I
- we

TARGETING WRITING SKILLS YR 5 © PASCAL PRESS ISBN 9781925726282

Structure of an imaginative historical setting

Heading

Although this example text has a heading, most descriptions occur as part of a longer text and will not always have a heading.

Circle the heading of the description.

Opening statements

The opening statements introduce the topic and the setting that will be described.

Highlight the opening statements that introduce the setting.

A series of sentences

A series of sentences names and describes the living conditions. Where the convicts lived and what was expected of them.

Circle the words and phrases that let you know that this setting is historical and not modern.
Write them here.

___

Concluding statement

A statement concludes the description and may include an evaluation of the setting.

Highlight the concluding statement. Underline the words and phrases in the concluding statement that provide an evaluation of the setting. List them here.

___

Language features of an imaginative historical setting

First-person narrator

This text is told from the point of view of the convict, Jane. She is the first-person narrator. She uses *I* to refer to herself, and *we* to refer to Ann, another convict, and herself.
If you were watching this scene, you would write about it in the third person. You would write *he*, *she*, or *they* or use their names.

Rewrite these sentences as if you were an onlooker, watching what happened.
Ann was in charge of cooking, while I washed and mended clothes. I washed in a nearby stream and draped clothes over rocks and bushes to dry.

We knew how lucky we were to be working for the sergeant.

___

___

Direct speech and reported speech

Direct speech refers to the exact words spoken by a character and is shown using speech marks at the beginning and end of the words spoken.
Example: *"You have been assigned to look after my family and lodgings," he said.*

A comma, question mark or exclamation mark separates the spoken words from the unspoken words that tell who the speaker is, for example, *he said*.

Reported or indirect speech reports what was said without using the exact words. Speech marks are not used.
Example: *The sergeant told Jane and Ann that they would be looking after his family.*

Rewrite this sentence as direct speech, the exact words that Jane may have said.

Jane knew how lucky she and Ann were to be working for the sergeant.

___

IMAGINATIVE TEXTS Writing a description of a historical setting

Before the narrator (Jane) arrived in Australia, she was imprisoned in London. The prisons were hulks, old ships that were no longer seaworthy and were used as floating prisons. Ann was in the same prison cell with Jane and many other unhappy prisoners.

Jane had stolen a loaf of bread from a baker because she and her brother were starving.

Ann had not yet returned a blanket she had borrowed to keep her sick mother warm.

Use the following words and phrases as a starting point to describe what it would have been like to be held in one of those prisons. Write your description in the first person, from Jane's point of view. Use some direct and reported speech to report what Jane and Ann may have said to each other.

- dark, damp, crowded, crammed
- old people, young people, children
- disease, illness
- poorly clothed, hungry, miserable, bleak
- for crimes like stealing a loaf of bread or a blanket
- smelt bad
- chained
- lots of rats

Plan

1 **Write a heading to identify your setting.**

2 **Write an opening statement to introduce your setting.**

3 **Think about Jane and Ann in the prison. What would they do? What would they think? What would they see? Smell? Feel? Wish? Write some phrases to describe the living conditions. Write from Jane's point of view using the pronouns *I* or *we*.**

4 **Direct speech**

What are some things Jane and Ann have said to each other about their living conditions? Write their words. Remember to use inverted commas.

5 **Write some action words to show what Jane and Ann did. Remember to use past tense.**

6 **Write a statement to conclude your description. Include an evaluation of the setting.**

 TARGETING WRITING SKILLS YR 5 © PASCAL PRESS ISBN 9781925726282

Draft

Now you are ready to write a draft of your description of an imaginative historical setting. Remember to:

- write your heading first
- write from Jane's point of view, a first-person narrator
- write an opening statement to introduce your setting
- describe what the living conditions were like
- use direct speech to record words that Jane and Ann said to each other. Remember to use inverted commas
- write a concluding statement that includes an evaluation of the setting
- write in sentences with capital letters and full stops.

First draft

Write a draft of your description of an imaginative historical setting here.

Feedback

Ask your teacher, classmates or someone at home to suggest what you could do to improve your description.

Revised draft

Self-evaluation

I wrote ☐ a heading on the first line.
☐ as a first-person narrator using the pronouns I and we.
☐ an opening statement to introduce the setting.
☐ a concluding statement with an evaluation of the setting.
☐ in sentences with capital letters and full stops.

I described ☐ the living conditions.
I used ☐ inverted commas to show direct speech.

PERSUASIVE TEXTS Exposition

The purpose of an exposition is to express an opinion and argue a case either for or against a topic.

Purpose: This text presents a personal point of view or opinion about single-use plastics.

Audience: The intended audience of this discussion is people who are interested to find out more about the uses of plastic.

Context: Texts like this would be found in school newsletters, newspapers, magazines and online.

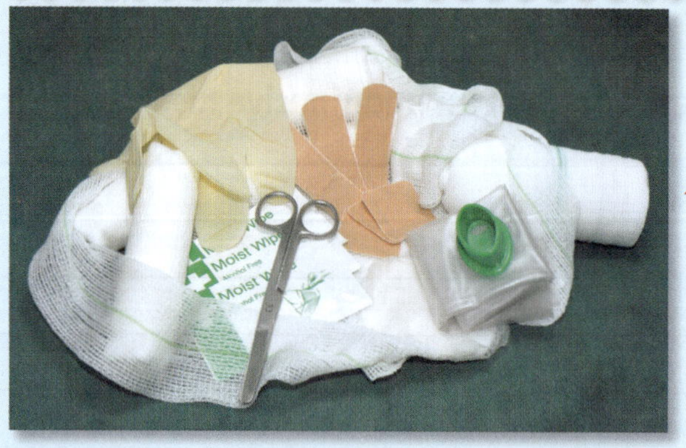

The persuasive text may be accompanied by a photograph or illustration.

A heading introduces the topic and point of view.

Opening statements attract attention and identify the point of view. (P)

A series of arguments is presented in separate paragraphs. The paragraphs provide evidence (E) and explain (E) reasons for holding the point of view.

A concluding statement reinforces the point of view by linking (L) back to the main argument.

Not All Single-Use Plastic is Bad

We are always being told to stop using single-use plastics because they are bad for the environment. However, sometimes single-use plastics are not only useful, but they are also essential.

It is crucial for health professionals to use single-use plastics to avoid the spread of infection. Scientists must also protect themselves and their materials with single-use plastics.

Moreover, plastic packaging is essential to keep food fresh and safe in emergencies, both locally and internationally.

Eco-friendly products are expensive. If people on low incomes had to buy them, then they would have to go without something else, maybe even food.

Single-use plastic products like bendable straws help people with disabilities to live independently. Many also rely on pre-cut food that is often packaged in plastic.

Yes, we can and should reduce our use of single-use plastics. However, we must also remember that there are times when single-use plastic is necessary.

Parts of Speech

Topic-related nouns and noun-groups
- plastic
- single-use plastics
- plastic packaging
- eco-friendly products

Present tense
- is
- are
- help
- can

Modal verbs
- must
- can
- should
- would

Emotive and evaluative words
- always
- bad
- useful
- essential
- crucial

Connectives
- however
- moreover
- also

TARGETING WRITING SKILLS YR 5 © PASCAL PRESS ISBN 9781925726282

Structure of an exposition

PEEL

An exposition is often written using what is known as the PEEL structure.

(P) The heading and opening statements of an exposition introduce the topic and point of view.

In this exposition, the heading is *Not All Single-Use Plastic is Bad*. The opening statements confirm this with, "sometimes single-use plastics are not only useful, but they are also essential." Readers know they will be finding out about situations in which single-use plastic is necessary.

1 Circle the heading of the persuasive text.

2 Underline the statements that introduce the point of view.

Evidence

A series of arguments provides evidence and explains reasons for the writer's point of view. Each argument is written in a separate paragraph.

(E) The first sentence in each paragraph provides the evidence.

3 Highlight the first sentence in each paragraph that provides the evidence.

Explain the evidence

(E) The sentences that follow the first evidence statement in each paragraph explain why the evidence is important.

4 Underline the sentences that explain the evidence.

Link back

(L) Each argument links back to the initial statement expressing the writer's point of view. You will see this by the repetition of *plastic* as either a noun or adjective in most paragraphs.

5 Circle each time *plastic* appears in the text.

The final statement also links back to the initial statement by restating and reinforcing the writer's position.

6 Highlight the final statement that reinforces the writer's position.

7 Sometimes arguments are presented using an *if ... then* structure. Rewrite the arguments in the text using the *if ... then* structure.

a If health professionals couldn't use single-use plastics, then ______________________________

____

b If food couldn't be packaged in plastic, then ______________________________

____

Language features of an exposition

Emotive and evaluative words

In an exposition, emotive and evaluative words are used to make the reader feel the same way about the topic as the writer does.

8 **a** Use a red pencil to circle all the emotive and evaluative words in the text.

b Write them here.

____

____

9 Write the argument that you find most convincing here.

____

Writing an exposition

Limit Screen Time for Young Children
Many people, including health professionals, have warned of the dangers of too much screen time for children.

Read these notes, then write an exposition that draws together all the points into one opinion.
Screen time includes time watching TV, playing electronic games and accessing games and other material on digital tablets and smartphones.

- ☐ less active
- ☐ less exercise
- ☐ less time playing with friends
- ☐ less time talking with family – delays language development
- ☐ only viewing, not actively engaged or thinking
- ☐ may lead to obesity and mental health issues
- ☐ become more focused on screen and less interested in world around them
- ☐ addictive
- ☐ changes sleep patterns – sleep less
- ☐ behaviour problems
- ☐ less time learning

Plan

1 **Write a heading that introduces the topic and point of view.** ______________________

____

2 **Write opening statements that attract attention and identify the point of view.**

____

____

3 a In the notes, tick ✓ the three arguments that you consider most important. Number them and highlight them.
b Use the same numbers to mark any statements that support those arguments. Circle them.

4 **Write a concluding statement that links back to your opening statement and reinforces your point of view.**

____

____

TARGETING WRITING SKILLS YR 5 © PASCAL PRESS ISBN 9781925726282

Draft

Now you are ready to write a draft of your exposition.
Remember to:

- write the title to introduce the topic
- (P) write opening statements to attract attention and identify your opinion
- (E) write short paragraphs to provide evidence for your opinion
- (E) write statements to explain why the evidence is important
- (L) restate your opinion and link your closing statement back to your opening statement
- use emotive words to influence the opinions of readers
- use capital letters at the beginning of sentences and full stops at the end.

First draft

Write a draft of your exposition here.

Feedback

Ask your teacher, classmates or someone at home to suggest what you could do to improve your exposition.

Revised draft

Self-evaluation

I wrote ☐ a title to identify the topic.
☐ (P) opening statements to identify my opinion.
☐ (E) short paragraphs giving evidence to support my opinion.
☐ (E) statements explaining why my evidence was important.
I restated ☐ (L) my opinion and linked my closing statement back to my opening statement.

I used ☐ emotive words.
☐ capital letters and full stops correctly.

TERM ONE

RECREATING TEXTS Imaginative description of a historical setting

The purpose of an imaginative description is to describe or give details about a character, place or object. A description of a place is called a setting and may include details about the living conditions at the time.

Purpose: The setting described in this poem, *The Old Bark School,* written by Henry Lawson in 1897, describes a bush school in the early days of European settlement of Australia.

Audience: The intended audience of the poem is people who enjoy reading poems about life in the bush in the early days of Australia.

Context: Poems like this would be found in books of poetry, anthologies, newspapers and magazines.

The Old Bark School

It was built of bark and poles, and the floor was full of holes
Where each leak in rainy weather made a pool;
And the walls were mostly cracks lined with calico and sacks,
There was little need for windows in the school.
Then we rode to school and back by the rugged gully-track,
On the old grey horse that carried three or four;
And he looked so very wise that he lit the master's eyes
Every time he put his head in at the door.
And we learnt the world in scraps from some ancient dingy maps
Long discarded by the public-schools in town;
And as nearly every book dated back to Captain Cook
Our geography was somewhat upside-down.

by Henry Lawson

Although the setting is described in poetry, it still follows some of the structure of a description in prose. A title identifies the setting. An opening statement introduces the setting.

1 **Circle the title.**

2 **Highlight the opening statement.**

A series of statements describes features of the setting, including the living conditions. In this poem, the living conditions refer to how they got to school and how they learned in school.

3 **Underline the words and phrases that describe the setting and the living conditions.**

4 **In your own words, not in poetry, write an opening statement to introduce the setting.**

____

____

TARGETING WRITING SKILLS YR 5 © PASCAL PRESS ISBN 9781925726282

Write an imaginative description of a historical setting

Use the information in the poem to write a description of the old bush school in your own words. Write your description in the first person, from the point of view of a student attending the school. Use some direct speech to record what the students and the teacher may have said to each other.

Remember to:

- write your heading first
- write from a student's point of view, a first-person narrator
- write an opening statement to introduce the setting
- describe features of the school and what the conditions were like for the students and teacher
- use direct speech to record words that the students and teacher may have said to each other. Remember to use inverted commas.
- write a concluding statement that includes an evaluation of the setting
- write in sentences with capital letters and full stops.

First draft

Write a draft of your historical description here.

Feedback

Ask your teacher, classmates or someone at home to suggest what you could do to improve your historical description.

Revised draft

Self-evaluation

I wrote
- ☐ a heading on the first line.
- ☐ as a first-person narrator using the pronouns I and we.
- ☐ an opening statement to introduce the setting.
- ☐ a concluding statement with an evaluation of the setting.
- ☐ in sentences with capital letters and full stops.

I described ☐ the living conditions.

I used ☐ inverted commas to show direct speech.

TERM 1 REVIEW

SENTENCES – Statements, questions, commands, exclamations

A **statement** is a sentence that gives information or an opinion.

A **question** is a sentence that asks for more information.

A **command** is a sentence that gives instructions or directions. It usually begins with a verb.

An **exclamation** expresses sudden surprise, joy or fright. It may or may not be a sentence.

1 Read the statements then rewrite them as a question (Q), command (C) and exclamation (E). Remember to use the correct punctuation.

The cyclist fitted new reflectors to her bike.

a (Q) ______________________________

b (C) ______________________________

c (E) ______________________________

2 Single-use plastic should be banned.

a (Q) ______________________________

b (C) ______________________________

c (E) ______________________________

Sentences can be made more interesting by expanding noun groups using adjectives.

3 Expand these sentences with noun groups to make the sentences more interesting.

a The student entered the school room.

____

b The cyclist rode down the road.

____

c The farmer saddled her horse.

____

d The whale swam in the water.

____

e The girl won the race.

____

INFORMATIVE TEXT – Explanation

An explanation explains how or why something in the world happens or how things work.

4 Use these notes to explain how a prism can be used to show that white light is made up of all the colours of the rainbow.

- prism – triangular block of glass or Perspex
- sunlight = white light
- colours have different wavelengths
- when white light enters the prism, it slows down, changes direction or bends (refracted)
- when it leaves the prism, different wavelengths (colours) go in different directions
- white light splits into different colours

____

____

____

____

TARGETING WRITING SKILLS YR 5 © PASCAL PRESS ISBN 9781925726282

IMAGINATIVE TEXT – Description of a historical setting

The purpose of an imaginative description of a setting is to describe or give details about a place and may include details about the living conditions at the time.

5 **Imagine you are a convict recently arrived in Australia. Describe your living conditions, including where you live, what you eat, how you are dressed and what you do. Make notes about these first.**

a Where do you live? ______________________

b What do you eat? ______________________

c What do you wear? ______________________

d What work do you do? ______________________

6 **Write your description in the first person, from the convict's point of view.**

____

____

____

____

PERSUASIVE TEXT – Exposition

The purpose of an exposition is to express opinions and argue a case either for or against a topic.

7 **Use these notes to convince others to stop using plastic toothbrushes and start using bamboo toothbrushes.**

Plastic toothbrushes take hundreds of years to break down.

Bamboo toothbrushes:

- clean teeth as well as plastic toothbrushes
- last as long as plastic toothbrushes
- are eco-friendly – handle can be put in the compost

Bamboo is:

- sustainable – grows quickly without fertilisers or pesticides
- biodegradable – decomposes naturally, doesn't pollute

a (P) Write your opinion as a heading.

____

b Write your most important argument as an *if ... then* statement.

____

c List emotive words you could use to influence the opinion of others.

____

8 **Write a persuasive text to convince others of your opinion.**

____

____

____

____

____

TERM TWO

GRAMMAR Compound sentences

A **clause** is a group of words with a subject and a verb. Sentences are constructed from clauses.

A **sentence** is a group of words that makes sense on its own. It always has a verb. It usually has a subject and often has an object.

A **simple sentence** has one independent, or main, clause and one verb.

Example: *Bike reflectors are made of plastic.*

A compound sentence has two independent clauses joined by a conjunction, such as for, and, nor, but, or, yet, so.

We can remember these conjunctions with the mnemonic, or memory aid, FANBOYS.

A comma is always written before the conjunction joining the two clauses.

Example: *Ann was in charge of cooking, and I was in charge of washing and mending.*

We can underline each of the independent clauses and circle the conjunction like this:

Ann was in charge of cooking, (and) I was in charge of washing and mending.

Use different colours to underline the independent clauses in these sentences. Circle the conjunction.

- **a** Very little rain falls in deserts, yet many living things survive there.
- **b** He missed the bus, so he had to walk to school.
- **c** The children could choose to watch a movie, or they could go to the beach.
- **d** Dragons are mythical creatures, and they often appear in fantasy stories.

Nor is used to join two negative clauses. The subject and verb are reversed in the clause following *nor*, and the verb is no longer negative.

Example: *I don't like putting my head under water, nor do I like getting my hair wet.*

The two simple sentences that were joined with *nor* were:

I don't like putting my head under water. I don't like getting my hair wet.

Rewrite these two simple sentences as one compound sentence using *nor*. Remember to reverse the subject and verb in the clause following *nor*. Remember to put a comma before *nor*.

- **a** The old man didn't go out very often. He didn't have many visitors.

  ____

- **b** The girl couldn't ride a skateboard. She couldn't ride a bike.

  ____

- **c** Humans don't have wings to fly. They don't have gills to breathe under water.

  ____

3 **Write the correct FANBOYS conjunction to join these clauses.**

- **a** I was feeling very hungry, __________ I didn't want to eat the leftover pizza.
- **b** He couldn't find his hat anywhere, __________ could he remember where he left it.
- **c** She made some cupcakes for the party, __________ she made some fruit punch too.
- **d** The boy wouldn't get on the roller-coaster, __________ he was feeling ill.
- **e** The children could have a party to celebrate, __________ they could go bowling.
- **f** The cinema was closed for renovations, __________ they went home.
- **g** Dragons might be scary, __________ children love to read about them.

TARGETING WRITING SKILLS YR 5 © PASCAL PRESS ISBN 9781925726282

Noun groups

Nouns name people, animals, places and objects. They name things we can see, hear, smell or touch. They also name thoughts and feelings.

A noun group helps to give more meaning to a noun. It usually begins with a **determiner**, for example, a, an, the, this, my, your, some.

A noun group may contain other words that give more information about the noun, including:

Adjectives: a *crunchy, red* apple; the *cross-country* race; the *long, dusty* road

Adjectival phrases: the girl *with brown eyes*; the boy *at the front of the line*

Clauses: the house *that Jack built*; the man *who lives down the road*

4 Circle the noun that is the subject of the sentence. Underline the words that form a noun group to give more information about it. Write (A) for adjective, (P) for adjectival phrase or (C) for clause.

☐ **a** The house at the bottom of the hill is vacant.

☐ **b** The author who visited our class lives in Sydney.

☐ **c** The huge, orange crabs live in the ocean.

☐ **d** The boy in the green shirt came first in the race.

5 Expand these sentences with noun groups to make them more interesting. Write (A) for adjective, (P) for adjectival phrase or (C) for clause to tell how you have expanded them.

a The boys are playing football.

☐ ____________________

b The bird flew onto the tree.

☐ ____________________

c The movie was very funny.

☐ ____________________

d The baby wouldn't stop crying.

☐ ____________________

Apostrophes: Possession

Apostrophes are used with nouns to show possession. When the noun is singular, *'s* is added.

Examples: *Zack's book; Dallas's father*

When the noun is plural and ends with *s*, just an apostrophe is added.

Examples: *the teachers' meeting; the Smiths' car*

6 Add the apostrophe in the correct place to these noun groups.

a a cats tail
b the neighbours pet
c the books cover
d Tinas friend
e the lions cages
f the principals office
g the teachers staffroom
h a giraffes neck
i Trazs brother

Apostrophes: Contractions

Apostrophes are used to mark a missing letter or letters when two words are combined.

Examples: *didn't = did not, wouldn't = would not, we'd = we would/had, it's = it is, she'll = she will*

7 Use different colours to match contractions to the words they replace.

can't	who's	hasn't	we're	should've	don't	here's
has not	do not	here is	can not	who is	we are	should have

INFORMATIVE TEXTS Information report

The purpose of an information report is to present factual information about a particular topic.

Purpose: This information report informs readers about Giant Spider Crabs and behaviour that helps their survival.

Audience: The intended audience of this information report is people who are interested in animals, their behaviour and how they adapt to their environment.

Context: Texts like this would be found in newspapers, science magazines and online.

Many information reports are accompanied by photographs.

A title identifies the topic.

Giant Spider Crabs

Opening statements provide general information about the topic.

Giant Spider Crabs grow up to 16 cm across their shell and 70 cm across their legs. They mostly live alone in ocean waters south of Australia.

However, during winter, huge groups gather in the shallower waters of Port Phillip Bay. The crabs climb on top of each other in piles up to 2 m high and over 100 m long.

Additional information is organised in a series of paragraphs around a main idea.

Like other crustaceans, Giant Spider Crabs have an exoskeleton, a hard external shell. The exoskeleton doesn't grow as our skin does. The crabs must shed their old shell (moult) to grow bigger.

It takes about an hour for a Giant Spider Crab to moult, but the soft new shell takes several days to harden. The legs are soft too, and walking is not easy. This makes it difficult to escape from predators.

Scientists think the Giant Spider Crabs gather and moult at the same time for safety. The chance of any individual crab being eaten is reduced.

A final paragraph concludes the report and links back to the opening statements.

After they have moulted, the Giant Spider Crabs return to deeper water.

Parts of Speech

Topic-related nouns, noun groups and technical language
- Giant Spider Crabs
- crabs
- crustaceans
- exoskeleton
- shell
- predators

Third person
- crabs
- they
- scientists

Present tense
- grow
- live
- climb
- have
- takes

Adverbial phrases
- during winter
- in the shallower waters
- from predators
- at the same time

TARGETING WRITING SKILLS YR 5 © PASCAL PRESS ISBN 9781925726282

Structure of an information report

Title

The title of an information report identifies the topic. Readers know that this information report is about Giant Spider Crabs.

Circle the title of the information report.

Opening statements

The opening statements provide general information to introduce the topic.

Highlight the opening statements that provide general information to introduce the topic.

A series of paragraphs

A series of paragraphs provides additional information. Each paragraph has one main idea.

Underline the main idea in each paragraph. In one or two words, list the main ideas below.

a ______________________ c ______________________

b ______________________ d ______________________

Final paragraph

The final paragraph concludes the report and links back to the opening statements.

a Highlight the final statement that concludes the report.

b Write the section of the opening statement that the final paragraph links to.

____

Language features of an information report

Topic nouns

Nouns are the names of things in our world such as people, places, animals and things.
In an information report, the nouns relate to the topic. They are **topic nouns**. **Technical language**, specific to the topic, may also be used.
Examples: *crustaceans, exoskeleton, predators*
Topic nouns are often repeated to link the text and ensure it can be understood.
Examples: *Giant Spider Crab, crab*

Circle *crab* each time it appears in the text.

To avoid too much repetition, sometimes pronouns and other words are used instead of always repeating *crab*.

Write other words that have been used instead of repeating *crab*.

____

Adverbial phrases

A **phrase** is a group of words that only makes sense in a sentence. It doesn't make sense on its own. It doesn't have a verb or a subject.
An **adverbial phrase** gives more information about a verb. It may tell how, when, where, why or for how long things happen.
Example: *'during winter'* tells when the huge groups gather.

Write the adverbial phrases that provide the following information.

a Where do the Giant Spider Crabs mostly live? ______________________

b Where do the crabs climb? ______________________

c Why must the crabs moult? ______________________

d How long does it take for a crab to moult? ______________________

e When do the Giant Spider Crabs gather and moult? ______________________

f Where do the crabs return after they have moulted? ______________________

FOCUS ON

INFORMATIVE TEXTS Writing an information report

Use the following notes to write an information report about how desert plants adapt to their environment.

How Desert Plants Adapt to their Environment

Some:

- store water in stems or leaves
- have no leaves or small leaves that only grow after rain – reduces water loss during photosynthesis
- have long root systems that spread deep and wide to find water
- live only for a short while and only produce seeds after rain (some seeds remain dormant for years)
- have leaves that turn throughout the day to reduce the surface exposed to the sun
- have a waxy coating – reduces water loss
- have flowers that only open at night when insects are more active

Many:

- have leaves with hairs on them – helps shade the plant and reduces water loss
- have spines or spikes – stops animals eating them for their water
- grow slowly and use less energy so need less water

Plan

1 Write a title for your information report.

___

2 Write a general statement to introduce the topic.

___

3 Decide on some main ideas around which you can organise the information into paragraphs, for example, leaves, shade or water storage. Write the main ideas here.

a ___
b ___
c ___
d ___

4 Use different colours to underline the statements you will include in each paragraph.

5 Write a concluding statement that links back to your opening paragraph.

___

 TARGETING WRITING SKILLS YR 5 © PASCAL PRESS ISBN 9781925726282

Draft

Now you are ready to write an information report about how desert plants adapt to their environment.

Remember to:

- write a title that identifies the topic
- write opening statements with general information to introduce the topic
- write a series of paragraphs, each organised around a main idea, to give more information about the topic
- write a final paragraph to conclude the report
- use adverbial phrases to tell how, when, where, why or for how long things happen
- write in sentences with capital letters and full stops.

First draft

Write a draft of your information report here.

Feedback

Ask your teacher, classmates or someone at home to suggest what you could do to improve your information report.

Revised draft

Self-evaluation

I wrote
- ☐ a title to identify the topic.
- ☐ opening statements with general information to introduce the topic.
- ☐ a series of paragraphs giving more information.
- ☐ a final paragraph to conclude the report.
- ☐ in sentences with capital letters and full stops.

I used ☐ adverbial phrases to tell how, when, where, why or for how long things happen.

I organised ☐ paragraphs around a main idea.

IMAGINATIVE TEXTS Description

The purpose of an imaginative description is to describe or give details about a character, place or object.

Purpose: This description describes or gives details about the characters and setting of a fantasy story.

Audience: The intended audience of this imaginative description is children who enjoy reading fantasy stories.

Context: Texts like this would be found in novels and stories in magazines. They do not usually occur on their own but form part of a longer text. Often the characters and setting are introduced at the same time. The purpose of an imaginative description is to describe or give details about a character, place or object.

A heading may be used to identify the setting.

Simpkins Meets the Dragon

Opening statements introduce the setting. The setting will be obvious by the words used and features described.

Simpkins thought he'd never been so frightened in all his life. And then he heard the slow whup, whup, whup of dragon wings and realised it was always possible to feel more fear. The beast was coming back. Simpkins grabbed a long, knobbly bone in each hand. He tried not to think about whose legs he was holding.

A series of sentences in one or more paragraphs describes the setting and introduces the location, the characters and the situation.

Whup, whup, whooomph. The huge dragon glided into the cave's entrance and began walking along the tunnel to his main lair. Simpkins could hear it snorting. The shuffle of claws on chalk changed to a clanking rattle as the dragon reached its lair.

A sudden flare of flame killed any thought Simpkins had of hiding. The cave lit up like his brothers' cottage when all its candles were lit. Simpkins hoisted the bones he was holding in what he hoped was a threatening pose.

When part of a longer text, the concluding statement may hint at what is to follow.

The dragon glared at him, a flame still flickering from its nostrils. "You dare to threaten me in my own lair?" it roared. "You humans have no respect!"

Parts of Speech

Topic-related nouns and noun groups
- a long, knobbly bone
- sudden flare of flame

Adjectives
- dragon
- huge
- main
- clanking

Similes
- like his brothers' cottage when all its candles were lit

Onomatopoeia
- whup, whup, whup

Past tense
- thought
- heard
- realised
- was
- grabbed

Apostrophes
- he'd
- cave's
- brothers'
- its

Source: Adapted from *The Way of the Dragon*, Sally Odgers, Blake Education.

TARGETING WRITING SKILLS YR 5 © PASCAL PRESS ISBN 9781925726282

Structure of an imaginative description – Fantasy setting

Heading

Although this example text has a heading, most descriptions occur as part of a longer text and will not always have a heading.

1 Circle the heading of the description.

Opening statements

The opening statements introduce the topic; the setting that will be described.

2
- a Highlight the opening statements that introduce the setting.
- b Circle the main word that lets you know that this is a fantasy setting.
- c Underline the words that tell you where the story takes place.

A series of sentences describes the setting

In this text, the setting introduces the location, the characters and the situation. There are two characters, Simpkins and the dragon.

3 Write words and phrases from the text that help describe the characters. Include physical characteristics and feelings.

a Simpkins: ______________________________

b The dragon: ______________________________

Concluding statement

The concluding statement may hint at what will happen next in the story.

4
- a Highlight the concluding statement.
- b Underline the words and phrases in the concluding statement that hint at what will happen next.

Language features of an imaginative description – Fantasy setting

Figurative language and sound devices

A **simile** compares two things using *like* or *as*. It gives more meaning to the text.
Example: *The cave lit up like his brothers' cottage when all its candles were lit.*

5 Write a simile to complete this sentence.

Simpkins was as scared as ______________________________.

Onomatopoeia

Onomatopoeia is a word or phrase that sounds like the word or phrase being described.
Examples: *whup, whup, whup; whup, whup, whooomph; clanking rattle*

6 Underline the examples of onomatopoeia in the text.

Apostrophes

Apostrophes are used with nouns to show possession. They are also used in contractions to mark a missing letter or letters when two words are combined.

7
- a Circle the words in the text that have an apostrophe.
- b List the words here. Write **(P)** for a word showing **possession** and **(C)** if it is a **contraction**. If it is a contraction, write the two words that have been combined.

____

Note: Read this sentence: 'The cave lit up like his brothers' cottage when all its candles were lit.' The word *its* refers to the cave's candles. It shows possession. However, it is a pronoun. Pronouns for possession don't have apostrophes. It's only correct to give *it's* an apostrophe when it's a contraction and means *it is*. The apostrophe shows that the *i* is missing.

Writing a description of a fantasy setting

Choose from these fantasy characters and settings, or choose your own, to write an encounter between the story hero and the fantasy character.

Characters:	Settings:	Situations:
dragon	mountains	searching for treasure
unicorn	forest	lost
fairy	desert	fighting for land
wizard	ocean	fulfilling a prophecy
warlock	castle	leading an army
giant	outer space	a quest
ogre	cave	overcoming a monster
leprechaun		saving someone
mermaid		
3-eyed monster		
genie		

Plan

1 In the list, circle the character or characters your story will be about. Write the characters, their names and one or two adjectives to describe them here.

a ______________________

b ______________________

2 Write some similes you could use to add interest to your descriptions of the characters.

a ______________________

b ______________________

3 Choose a setting. Circle it in the list. Write words to describe the setting here.

____

4 Choose a situation your hero will be involved in when the fantasy character is encountered. Circle it in the text and briefly describe it here.

____

5 Think of some action words you might use in describing the situation. List them here.

____

6 Write some onomatopoeia words you could use to describe the action.

____

7 Write a heading for your description.

____

8 Write an opening statement to introduce the setting, including the characters and the situation.

____

____

 TARGETING WRITING SKILLS YR 5 © PASCAL PRESS ISBN 9781925726282

Draft

Now you are ready to write a draft of your description of a fantasy setting. Remember to:

- give your description a heading
- write opening statements to introduce the fantasy setting
- write a series of paragraphs to describe the setting, including the characters, the location and the situation
- use onomatopoeia to describe some of the action
- use similes to describe features of the characters and location
- write in sentences with capital letters and full stops.

First draft

Write a draft of your description of a fantasy setting here.

Feedback

Ask your teacher, classmates or someone at home to suggest what you could do to improve your description.

Revised draft

Self-evaluation

I wrote
- ☐ a heading on the first line.
- ☐ opening statements to introduce the setting.
- ☐ a series of paragraphs describing the setting, including the characters, the location and the situation.
- ☐ in sentences with capital letters and full stops.

I used
- ☐ onomatopoeia to describe some of the action.
- ☐ similes to describe features of the characters and location.

Advertising exposition

An advertisement is a type of exposition. The purpose of advertisements is to promote goods, services or activities to persuade people to choose them. They use positive words and images, are often visually appealing and use catchy slogans.

Purpose: This advertisement aims to persuade people to purchase Greenline Skateboards.

Audience: The intended audience is young people who care about the environment and want a fun activity or method of transport that doesn't harm the environment.

Context: Texts like this would be found in newspapers, magazines and online, especially those that target a young audience.

Advertisements are often illustrated with photos, cartoons or diagrams to catch the reader's attention.

A bold heading to catch attention.

New! Environmentally-friendly Greenline Skateboards

Need an incentive to get off your screens and outside in the fresh air? A Greenline Skateboard is exactly what you need.

Skateboarding — the healthy alternative — have fun, get fit and reduce your carbon footprint all at the same time.

Needing no battery, using no petrol and made from 100% recycled materials, the new Greenline Skateboards are completely harmless to the environment and safe for skaters of all ages.

Whether you skate alone or with friends; just for thrills or cruising around town, Greenline Skateboards are the perfect choice. We've got a Greenline deck to suit every taste.

Wheels with grip and stability will have you hopping curbs, grinding rails and mastering ollie tricks in no time.

World champion Keegan Falcon says, "I wouldn't trust any other. Greenline's the only skateboard for me."

Get your skates on with a Greenline Skateboard now. Available at all reputable stores where skateboards are sold, on the street and online. Mention this ad for a whopping 25% discount.

Rhetorical questions gain interest.

Paragraphs are short and use simple language to appeal to potential customers and explain why their product is best.

It speaks directly to the audience – you.

Parts of Speech

Topic-related nouns and noun groups
- Greenline Skateboard
- Environment
- skaters
- deck
- tricks

Personal pronouns
- your
- you
- we
- I
- me

Emotive words and superlatives
- incentive
- exactly
- need
- healthy
- 100% recycled
- completely harmless
- perfect

 TARGETING WRITING SKILLS YR 5 © PASCAL PRESS ISBN 9781925726282

✲ Structure of an advertising exposition

An advertising exposition, or advertisement, speaks directly to the audience and is written in strong emotive language that gets straight to the point. Although advertisements may vary in layout, they usually include features that are common to other persuasive texts.

Bold heading

In an advertisement, a bold heading is used to catch the attention and inform the reader of what is being advertised.

1 Highlight the heading of the advertisement.

Rhetorical question

A rhetorical question doesn't require an answer. It speaks directly to the audience and is used to gain interest.

2 Underline the rhetorical question.

Arguments for the product

Each paragraph provides the audience with reasons for choosing the advertised product.

3
- **a** Underline the statements that provide reasons for choosing a Greenline Skateboard.
- **b** Write the reasons people may choose Greenline Skateboards here.

____

____

Celebrity endorsement

Endorsements by celebrities are often used in an effort to convince potential customers.

4 Circle the celebrity endorsement.

Incentive

Advertisements often end with an incentive, calling potential customers to take action and make a purchase now.

5 Highlight the incentive that calls potential customers to take action and purchase now.

✲ Language features of an advertising exposition

Emotive words and superlatives

In an advertisement, emotive words and superlatives, like *best* and *perfect*, are used to convince the potential customer to become an actual customer. They may exaggerate the product's benefits to snare a sale.

Consider this statement: *Skateboarding is a fun activity*. It is not very compelling.

6 The same message is repeated at least three times in the text. Write the statements here. Circle the superlatives and emotive words that try to convince you to buy a Greenline product.

- **a** ____
- **b** ____
- **c** ____

7 Read the following statement. Suggest an alternative way of saying the same thing using stronger emotive and superlative words.

Shorts come in a range of colours.

____

____

PERSUASIVE TEXTS Advertising exposition

Write an advertisement to persuade others to purchase a game you enjoy or a product you think is good. Convince your young audience that the item will promote health and not harm the environment.

Note: As with the advertisement for Greenline Skateboards, it is not necessary for either the product or the celebrity to be real.

Plan

1. **Draw or paste a picture of the item you are advertising in the box.**

2. **Choose a catchy name for your product.** ______________________

3. **What age group will be interested in your product?** ______________________

   This is the target audience for your advertisement. If the audience is very young, you will need to include their parents in the audience as well.

4. **Write a bold heading to catch the attention of your audience. Include the product name.**

   ____

5. **List benefits of your product, including benefits to health and the environment.**

   ____

6. **Choose the benefit that will have the most appeal to your audience and write a rhetorical question about it.**

   ____

7. **Think of a celebrity who might endorse your product and what they might say about it. Write the endorsement. Remember to use inverted commas to show the words that the celebrity says.**

   ____

8. **List places where your product can be purchased.**

   ____

9. **Write an incentive that will encourage your audience to take action and purchase your product now.**

   ____

10. **List emotive words and superlatives that you can use to convince your audience about the benefits of your product.**

    ____

TARGETING WRITING SKILLS YR 5 © PASCAL PRESS ISBN 9781925726282

Draft

Now you are ready to write a draft of your advertisement.
Remember to:

- write a bold, catchy heading that includes the product name
- write a rhetorical question to create interest in your product
- write short paragraphs about each of the benefits of your product
- include benefits of your product on health and the environment
- use emotive words and superlatives to convince readers of the benefits of your product
- include a celebrity endorsement
- include an incentive to encourage your audience to buy your product now.

First draft

Write a draft of your advertisement here.

Feedback

Ask your teacher, classmates or someone at home to suggest what you could do to improve your advertisement.

Revised draft

Self-evaluation

I wrote
- ☐ a bold, catchy heading.
- ☐ a rhetorical question to create interest.
- ☐ short paragraphs about the benefits of the product.

I included
- ☐ benefits on health and the environment.
- ☐ a celebrity endorsement.
- ☐ an incentive to buy now.

I used
- ☐ emotive words and superlatives.
- ☐ capital letters and full stops correctly in sentences.

UNIT 16 FOCUS ON

RECREATING TEXTS Persuasive text – Advertising exposition

An advertisement is a type of exposition. The purpose of advertisements is to promote goods, services or activities to persuade people to choose them. They use positive words and images, are often visually appealing and use catchy slogans.

Purpose: This advertisement aims to persuade people that their brand of fast food is a healthy option.

Audience: The intended audience is families who are short of time and want to purchase takeaway fast-food meals that provide healthy options.

Context: Texts like this would be found in newspapers, magazines and brochures, and catalogues that are delivered to mailboxes. They may also be found on restaurant websites.

Imagine you own a fast-food restaurant that serves healthy food. Use information from this article in an advertisement encouraging people to order food to take away from your restaurant.

Not All Fast Food is Bad

Food is essential to keep our bodies healthy and full of energy.

Junk food is not real food. It is called junk food as it contains very little nutritional value. It doesn't have the vitamins, protein or fibre that our bodies need. What it usually does contain is lots of salt, fat, sugar and even chemicals. Too much of any of these things will not keep us healthy.

Fast food may not be junk food. Fast food is food that is ready in a hurry. It has been prepared to save you time. Many fast-food companies produce low-fat, low-sugar foods, and many restaurants offer takeaway service for tasty, healthy meals.

Fast food can be good for you if you choose foods with good nutritional value and eat junk food only rarely.

Plan

1. In the text, underline the benefits of healthy takeaway food.
2. What type of food will you sell at your restaurant? ______________________
3. What is the catchy name of your restaurant? ______________________
4. List benefits to customers of buying takeaway food from your restaurant.

   ____

   ____

   ____

   ____
5. Choose the benefit that will have most appeal to your audience and write a rhetorical question about it.

   ____
6. Write an incentive that will encourage your audience to take action and order now.

   ____
7. List emotive words and superlatives you can use to convince your audience about the benefits of buying and eating your food.

   ____

TARGETING WRITING SKILLS YR 5 © PASCAL PRESS ISBN 9781925726282

Write a persuasive text – Advertising exposition

Write an advertisement to convince readers to choose your restaurant's takeaway food because it is good for them.

Remember to:

- write a bold, catchy heading that includes the name of your restaurant
- write a rhetorical question to create interest in your restaurant's takeaway food
- write short paragraphs about the benefits of choosing your food
- use emotive words and superlatives to convince readers your takeaway food is the best
- include a celebrity endorsement
- include an incentive to encourage your audience to buy your product now.

First draft

Write a draft of your advertisement here.

Feedback

Ask your teacher, classmates or someone at home to suggest what you could do to improve your advertisement.

Revised draft

Self-evaluation

I wrote ☐ a bold, catchy heading.
☐ a rhetorical question to create interest.
☐ short paragraphs about the benefits of choosing my food.

I used ☐ emotive words and superlatives.
☐ capital letters and full stops correctly in sentences.

I included ☐ a celebrity endorsement.
☐ an incentive to buy now.

COMPOUND SENTENCES

A **compound sentence** has two independent clauses joined by a conjunction, such as for, and, nor, but, or, yet, so (FANBOYS). A comma is always written before the conjunction joining the two clauses.

1 Write the correct FANBOYS conjunction to join these clauses.

- **a** Giant Spider Crabs moult in one hour, __________ the new shell takes days to harden.
- **b** The desert looks dry and barren, __________ many plants survive there.
- **c** Simpkins was frightened, __________ he picked up a long, knobbly bone in each hand.
- **d** The princess was braver than a knight, __________ she defeated the monster dragon.
- **e** Fast food is not always bad for you, __________ is it always junk food.
- **f** You could buy this unhealthy junk food, __________ you could buy this healthy fast food.
- **g** Giant Spider Crabs are not the biggest in the world, __________ they are still very big.

2 Expand these sentences with noun groups to make them more interesting. Write (A) for adjective, (P) for adjectival phrase or (C) for clause to tell how you have expanded them.

a Crabs live in the ocean.

☐ ____

b The dragon entered the cave.

☐ ____

c The children rode their skateboards down the hill.

☐ ____

d This burger is the best I've ever tasted.

☐ ____

INFORMATIVE TEXT – Information report

An information report presents factual information about a particular topic.

3 Use these notes to write an information report about the oldest living trees. Remember to give your report a heading.

- a Great Basin bristlecone pine – named Methuselah – in California USA – over 4,800 years old
- a Patagonian cypress – named Alerce Milenario or Gran Abuelo (names that mean great-grandfather) – in Chile – may be over 5,000 years old
- oldest tree in Australia – Huon pine – Tasmania – about 2,000 years old
- age of trees is estimated using tree-ring data – before Egyptians built the pyramids
- concern for their survival as the climate changes – water dries up – bushfires

____

____

____

____

____

TARGETING WRITING SKILLS YR 5 © PASCAL PRESS ISBN 9781925726282

IMAGINATIVE TEXT – Description

The purpose of an imaginative description is to describe or give details about a character, place or object.

4 **Write a description of this fantasy character. Remember to describe each of its features. Use similes and metaphors to make your description more interesting.**

____

____

____

____

____

____

____

____

PERSUASIVE TEXT – Advertising exposition

The purpose of an advertisement is to promote goods, services or activities to persuade people to choose them.

People often say they would like their hair to be anything other than what it is.

If it's curly, they want straight. If it's straight, they want curly. If it's long, they want short; or they want long if it's short.

You have designed a product that will give everyone the hairstyle they want. Not only that, it's environmentally friendly too.

5 **Write an advertisement to convince customers to purchase your product.**

GRAMMAR Complex sentences

A **clause** is a group of words with a subject and a verb. Sentences are constructed from clauses.

A **sentence** is a group of words that makes sense on its own. It always has a verb. It usually has a subject and often has an object.

A **simple sentence** has just one independent, or main, clause and one verb.

A **compound sentence** has two independent clauses joined by a conjunction.

A **complex sentence** is also constructed from two or more clauses. The clauses make connections between ideas.

In a complex sentence, there is one clause that tells the main idea. It is called the **main clause** or the **principal clause**. It makes sense on its own.

A **subordinate** or **dependent clause** gives more information about the main idea in the principal clause. Subordinate or dependent clauses may not make sense on their own.

Subordinate clauses are linked to the principal clause by a conjunction or a relative pronoun.

Conjunctions often used to join subordinate clauses:

after	when	although	so	because	before
wherever	since	whenever	as	once	where
though	while	until	if	unless	whilst

Relative pronouns:

who	whom	whose	which	that

The conjunction or relative pronoun is at the beginning of the subordinate clause. A subordinate clause can occur at the beginning, the end or in the middle of a sentence. When it is in the middle of a sentence, it is called an **embedded clause**.
Example: *The Giant Spider Crabs, so scientists think, gather in groups to moult.*

Complex sentences may link ideas by providing a **reason** or **purpose**.
Example: *He ran home fast because his grandfather was coming over.*

The subordinate clauses answer the question 'why'.

Read these complex sentences. In each sentence, highlight the subordinating conjunction, circle the verbs in each clause, underline the main clause in green and underline the subordinate clause in red.

Example: He ran home fast because his grandfather was coming over.

- **a** I went to the doctor because I hurt my foot during soccer.
- **b** I got my foot x-rayed so the doctor could see the damage.
- **c** The entire school crammed into the hall because the principal was making an announcement.
- **d** Since it was raining, our excursion was cancelled.
- **e** The bus drivers were on strike as they wanted safer buses.

 TARGETING WRITING SKILLS YR 5 © PASCAL PRESS ISBN 9781925726282

GRAMMAR Complex sentences

Complex sentences may link ideas by expressing a condition or a concession.

Examples: *It won't work anymore if you remove the plug.*
It won't work unless you turn it on.

Read these complex sentences. In each sentence, highlight the subordinating conjunction, circle the verbs in each clause, underline the main clause in green and underline the subordinate clause in red.

Examples: It won't work anymore if you remove the plug.
It won't work unless you turn it on.

- **a** Unless your scores improve, you won't make it into the team.
- **b** Although they are mythical creatures, dragons are quite beautiful.
- **c** The river will flood again if it doesn't stop raining.
- **d** The students were told to stay home if they were unwell.
- **e** I won't make it to practice on time unless the bus arrives soon.

Complex sentences may link ideas by expressing a **time relationship**.

Examples: *We had to stay inside while the storm was raging.*
Whenever there is a storm, we have to stay inside.

Read these complex sentences. In each sentence, highlight the subordinating conjunction, circle the verbs in each clause, underline the main clause in green and underline the subordinate clause in red.

Examples: We can't go home until the storm has passed.
Whenever there is a storm, we have to stay inside.

- **a** The children had pizza after the game was over.
- **b** I was feeling excited about the concert before I knew we were going.
- **c** We always go to the park when my cousins come over.
- **d** Whenever we go to the zoo, we always feed the kangaroos first.
- **e** We must do our best until it is the last day of school.

Add subordinate clauses to give more details about these simple sentences. Use one of the conjunctions from the box. Use as many different conjunctions as you can.

- **a** I will make breakfast on Sunday ______________________.
- **b** We always go to the cinema ______________________.
- **c** I was late for school ______________________.
- **d** This bicycle is the best ______________________.
- **e** The tablet will not work ______________________.
- **f** My mum drives carefully ______________________.
- **g** The farmer takes the horse to the vet ______________________.
- **h** The soccer player can't play again ______________________.
- **i** The bridge was built over the river ______________________.
- **j** The jug was empty ______________________.

The purpose of a procedure is to give instructions, explain how to do something, tell how to get somewhere, or explain the rules to be followed.

Purpose: This procedure explains how to make a refracting telescope.

Audience: The intended audience of this procedure is children who are learning about light or space, or just like to have fun making things.

Context: Texts like this would be found in children's magazines, and online.

A procedure may include a photograph or illustrations to improve understanding.

A title identifies the purpose of the instructions.

An introductory statement may also be used to explain the goal or objective.

Items required to complete the procedure are listed. Bullet points are often used.

Subheadings are used for each section.

Each instruction is written as a command with the verb at the beginning. The subject 'you' is said to be understood.

A series of numbered steps tells what to do in order.

Make a Refracting Telescope

A refracting telescope uses two magnifying glasses to bend light and bring it into focus. For this to work, you need to find the length between two lenses that brings the image into focus. This is called finding the focal length.

Materials

- a long cardboard tube
- 1 magnifying glass, about 1 cm diameter
- 1 magnifying glass, about 3 cm diameter
- scissors
- adhesive tape
- a ruler
- a book with writing

Steps

1. Hold the larger magnifying glass over the writing. Put the smaller magnifying glass between the bigger glass and your eye.
2. Move the smaller magnifying glass closer or further away from the larger glass until the writing is clear. The print will be upside down.
3. Measure the distance between the two glasses. This will be the focal length of your telescope.
4. Tape the magnifying glasses inside the cardboard tube with the focal length between them.
5. Look at the night sky with your refracting telescope.

Parts of Speech

Topic-related nouns and noun groups

- refracting telescope
- magnifying glasses
- lenses
- focal length
- cardboard tube
- adhesive tape

Action verbs – Present tense

- hold
- put
- move
- measure
- tape
- look

Prepositional phrases

- over the writing
- between the bigger glass and your eye
- from the larger glass
- inside the cardboard tube

Source: *Exploring Space, Go Facts,* Blake Education.

TARGETING WRITING SKILLS YR 5 © PASCAL PRESS ISBN 9781925726282

Structure of a procedure

Title

The title of a procedure identifies the purpose of the instructions. It tells readers what the instructions refer to.

The title of this procedure is 'Make a Refracting Telescope'. Readers know they will be reading the instructions for making a refracting telescope.

Circle the title of the procedure.

Introductory statements

Introductory statements may be used to explain the goal or objective.

Underline the statements that explain the goal or objective of the activity.

Subheadings

Subheadings are used to organise the information. There are two subheadings in this procedure.

a Highlight the subheadings.
b Write them here.

____

Language features of a procedure

Commands and action verbs

A command is a sentence that tells you what to do. It usually begins with a verb telling you the action you need to take.

In a command, the subject is left out. The subject is said to be understood. We know it is 'you'.

Example: *(You) Hold the larger magnifying glass over the writing.*

a Reread the text. Draw a box around the action words that begin each command telling you what to do.
b Write the action words here.

____

Prepositional phrases

A **phrase** is a group of words that only makes sense in a sentence. It doesn't make sense on its own. It doesn't have a verb and it doesn't have a subject.

A **prepositional phrase** usually begins with a preposition and tells where a person or object is in space or time.

Example: *between* the bigger glass and your eye

In a procedure, prepositional phrases are necessary to tell where and when things should occur. If the *where* and *when* aren't followed, the procedure may not work as planned.

a Read the steps of the procedure. Highlight the prepositional phrases that tell you where or when to carry out the actions.
b Write the prepositions that begin each phrase here.

____

6 Write prepositional phrases to complete these sentences.

a Kick the ball ______________________________.
b Be at school ______________________________.
c Write your name ______________________________.
d Put your book ______________________________.

INFORMATIVE TEXTS Writing instructions for making a model of a solar eclipse

Use this image and explanation of what happens in a solar eclipse to write the procedure for making a model to demonstrate a solar eclipse on the part of Earth where you live.

Sometimes the Moon moves between the Sun and the Earth so that the three are in a straight line. The Moon blocks the Sun's light, and part of the Earth is in the Moon's shadow. This is a solar eclipse.

Plan

1 a Write a title for your procedure. ______________________________

b Write a statement to explain the goal or objective of your procedure.

____

2 **List the equipment that is required.**

____

____

____

3 **List the action words that you will use to tell others what to do.**

____

____

____

____

4 **Write the prepositional phrases that will help make your explanations clear.**

____

____

____

____

____

5 **List the steps that need to be followed to demonstrate a solar eclipse on the part of Earth where you live.**

1 ______________________________

2 ______________________________

3 ______________________________

4 ______________________________

5 ______________________________

 TARGETING WRITING SKILLS YR 5 © PASCAL PRESS ISBN 9781925726282

Draft

Now you are ready to write a procedure for making a model to demonstrate a solar eclipse on the part of Earth where you live.

Remember to:

- write a title for your procedure
- write an introductory statement to explain the goal or objective of your procedure
- use subheadings for each section
- list the items required and use bullet points
- write commands to explain what to do and number the instructions
- use present tense
- write in sentences with capital letters and full stops.

First draft

Write a draft of your procedure here.

Feedback

Ask your teacher, classmates or someone at home to suggest what you could do to improve your procedure.

Revised draft

Self-evaluation

I wrote
- ☐ a title to identify the procedure.
- ☐ an introductory statement to explain the goal or objective of the procedure.
- ☐ commands to explain what to do.
- ☐ in present tense.
- ☐ in sentences with capital letters and full stops.

I used
- ☐ subheadings for each section.
- ☐ bullet points to list items required.

I numbered
- ☐ the commands in order.

IMAGINATIVE TEXTS Dramatic play

A play is a narrative that has been written for a dramatic performance.

Purpose: This dramatic play entertains with an amusing story about a genie who grants wishes.

Audience: The intended audience of this dramatic play is children.

Context: This play is part of a longer story. Stories like this would be found in anthologies and magazines for children, in books of plays or as a chapter of a longer story.

Punctuation
A lot of punctuation is used to tell actors what expression to use.

Direct speech
The words are the exact words spoken by the actors. However, inverted commas are not used in a play.

A play may be illustrated to aid interest and meaning.

The title introduces the topic or setting of the play.

The characters are listed.

Plays are divided into sections called Acts. Acts are divided into smaller sections called scenes. A scene is like a chapter in a book. The scene may be described as part of the orientation.

Genie in a Teapot

Characters: Ryan, Pritesh, Stall owner, Genie

ACT 1

SCENE 1 (*at a car boot sale*)

RYAN: How much have we made?

PRITESH: (*counts the money*) Twenty-one dollars and fifty cents — that's ten dollars each.

RYAN: Um, ten dollars and seventy-five cents!

PRITESH: Time to pack up then.

RYAN: (*Ryan sees a teapot on another stall.*) Hey, look at that teapot!

PRITESH: Gross or what!

RYAN: I know my Nan would love it! She loves gold stuff like that.

RYAN: (*speaking to the stall owner*) How much is the teapot?

STALL OWNER: One dollar fifty.

RYAN: Done! (*pays the stall owner*)

PRITESH: You've been done mate.

Later

PRITESH: What's going on? Everything you wish for is coming true. (*sees smoke coming from the teapot*) And look! What's happening to your teapot?

GENIE: (*smoke disappears and a giant gold genie appears.*) I am a genie!

RYAN: A ... a genie? You mean like a genie of the ... teapot?

GENIE: Yes, Master.

Characters' names are capitalised when they speak. There is a new line for each speaker.

Stage directions are written in italics to tell players where to look or what to do. Actors do not say those words.

A resolution concludes the scene, but it may not be the conclusion of the entire story.

Parts of Speech

First and second person as characters speak to each other
- we
- I
- you

Proper nouns (capitals)
- Ryan
- Pritesh
- Genie

Present tense
- look
- know
- loves
- is
- am

Source: Adapted from *The Car Boot Genie*, Jillian Powell, Blake Education.

Structure of a dramatic play

Title

A play is an imaginative narrative. It has a title that provides a clue as to what the story is about. The title of this play *Genie in a Teapot* lets the reader know that this story will involve a genie and is a fantasy story.

Circle the title of the play.

Orientation

The list of characters and the description of the scene provide information about the setting.

Complete these details about the story.

a Who is the story about? ______________________________

b When does the story take place? ______________________________

c Where does the story take place? ______________________________

Complication

The complication is a problem that affects one or more of the characters.

What is the complication in this story?

____

Resolution

The resolution occurs when the problem is solved.

How is the problem solved in this part of the story?

____

Language features of a dramatic play

Stage directions

Stage directions tell the characters where they should be and what they should do. Stage directions are written in *italics*. Actors do not say the stage directions out loud.

Underline all the stage directions, italicised words, you see in the play.

Direct speech

Direct speech refers to the actual words spoken by a character. It is also called dialogue. In a story, dialogue, or direct speech, is shown by placing **speech marks** or **inverted commas** ("__") around the words spoken. However, in a play, the exact words spoken by a character are written alongside the character's name. Inverted commas are not used. The character's name is written in capital letters.

Choose one of the characters as if you were to take the part of that character in the play.

a Circle the name of the character each time it is listed with something to say.

b Highlight the words that the character says. Remember, they do not say the stage directions out loud. Do not highlight the italicised words.

Punctuation

Punctuation is important in a play. It tells the characters what expression to use. Question marks tell them to use a questioning expression. Exclamation marks tell them to be surprised, alarmed or to shout. Ellipsis points (...) tell the character to pause.

Reread the words that your character says. Circle the punctuation marks.

UNIT 21 FOCUS ON IMAGINATIVE TEXTS

Writing a dramatic play

Read this scene from *Car Boot Genie*. Rewrite it as a play.

I Wish

Ryan and Pritesh visit Nan at her home.
"Now then, what do we have here?" Nan asked.
"It's a present," Ryan said. "I hope you like it."
He gave Nan the teapot.
"Oh Ryan, it's lovely," Nan said, holding up the pot.
Ryan gave Pritesh a look that said, "I told you so."
"You are good boys," Nan said. "You know what I wish?"
"What's that, Nan?" said Ryan, watching the teapot.
"I wish I could win that lottery so I could really treat you both."
Just then there was a ring at the doorbell.
"Now who's that?" Nan said.
Ryan looked at Pritesh.
"Mrs Walker?" they heard a man say. "I have some very good news for you."

Source: Adapted from *Car Boot Genie*, Jillian Powell, Blake Education.

Plan

1 **Title: What is the title of your play?**

____

2 **Characters: List the characters who appear in the story.**

____

3 **Setting: Where does the story take place?**

____

4 **Stage directions: Think about some stage directions that might be required. Write them here.**

____

____

5 **Direct speech:**

a Using a different colour for each character, highlight the words that each character says.

b Choose one of the characters. Write the words the character speaks here. Remember to write the character's name in capital letters. Do not use inverted commas. Use punctuation to let the player know what expression should be used.

____

____

____

____

Draft

Now you are ready to write a draft of your imaginative dramatic play.
Remember to:

- write the title of the play first
- list the characters who appear in the play
- number and describe the scene (setting)
- write the names of speakers in capital letters
- begin each different speaker on a new line, and do not use inverted commas
- write stage directions to tell actors where to look, what is happening or what to do
- use punctuation so that actors know what expression to put into the words they say.

First draft

Write a draft of your dramatic play here.

Feedback

Ask your teacher, classmates or someone at home to suggest what you could do to improve your dramatic play.

Revised draft

Self-evaluation

I wrote ☐ the title of the play first.
☐ the names of speakers in capital letters.
I used ☐ stage directions to tell actors where to look, what happened or what to do.
☐ punctuation so that actors would know how to express the words.
I listed ☐ the characters in the play.
I numbered ☐ and described the scene (setting).
I started ☐ a new line for each speaker.
I did not use ☐ inverted commas.

PERSUASIVE TEXTS Review of a video game

The purpose of a review of a video game is to summarise what happens in the game and present an objective opinion about it. The writer may share their own (subjective) thoughts or feelings about it, but also take into account the opinions of others.

Purpose: This text reviews the video game, Minecraft.

Audience: The intended audience of this video game review is others who enjoy video games and may be looking for the next video game to play.

Context: Texts like this would be found in newspapers and magazines, and online.

A review of a video game may be accompanied by an image from the game.

A heading identifies the name of the video game. Each word is capitalised.

Minecraft

Opening statements identify the opinion of the game and provide general information about it.

Minecraft is one of the most popular video games of all time. It is both fun and educational. It is easy to learn and suitable for players over 8 years. It can be played on computers, game consoles, phones, tablets and even some televisions.

One or more paragraphs explain what the game is about and how it is played.

There is no story in Minecraft. Players build their own worlds using 3D blocks. While it may look simple at first, it becomes more complex as players progress. They use problem-solving skills and creativity to design and make their scenes. They can make anything from single buildings to farms, villages, cities and entire worlds. The only limit is their imagination.

Players can choose between survival mode and creative mode. In survival mode, they have to build shelter and find food to stay healthy. They may even meet monsters to battle, but the monsters aren't scary. In creative mode, players can create whatever they want. There are no monsters in creative mode.

A concluding statement sums up the opinion of the game and links back to the opening statement.

Minecraft is a fun game for anyone who likes to develop their thinking skills. Some say it can even help you become smarter.

Parts of Speech

Topic-related nouns and non-groups
- games
- computers
- game consoles
- blocks
- players
- imagination
- skills

Third person
- Minecraft
- Players
- they
- some

Present tense
- is
- can
- use

Emotive words and superlatives
- most popular
- fun and educational
- easy
- complex
- limit
- smarter

TARGETING WRITING SKILLS YR 5 © PASCAL PRESS ISBN 9781925726282

Structure of a review of a video game

Heading

The heading identifies the name of the video game to be reviewed. Each word of the name is capitalised.

1 a Circle the name of the video game.
b Highlight the capital letter.

Opening statements

The opening statements identify the opinion of the game and provide general information about it, including the age group it is suitable for and what is required to play it.

2 a Highlight the statement that identifies the opinion of the game.
b Highlight the age group the game is suitable for.
c Underline what is required for playing the game.
d Highlight the benefits mentioned to persuade the reader to choose Minecraft.

About the game

One or more paragraphs tell what the game is about and how it is played.

3 **Circle the paragraphs that tell what the game is about and how it is played.**
In each of these paragraphs, the writer mentions aspects or benefits of the game that may convince the reader to choose it.

4 **Highlight the aspects and benefits.**

5 **Highlight the words in the concluding statement that link back to the opening statement.**

Language features of a video game review

Objective opinions

In this video game review, the writer is not just giving their own personal or subjective opinion. The writer is expressing an opinion held by many others, an objective opinion.

Example: The writer does not say, "I think Minecraft is the best game ever."

The writer steps back from their own opinion to write: "Minecraft is one of the most popular video games of all time."

6 **Rewrite this objective opinion as a personal opinion.**
Some say it can even help you become smarter.

____

Emotive words and superlatives

Emotive words and superlatives are used to convince the reader to feel the same way about the video game as the writer does even if it appears the writer may not be expressing a personal opinion.

7 **List words and phrases the writer uses to convince the reader to choose Minecraft.**

____

____

PERSUASIVE TEXTS — Writing a review of a video game

Write a review to tell others about a video game you enjoy playing. Write the review from an objective, rather than subjective, point of view. Although you may be telling the readers what you think of the game and why, and why they should play it, you will be writing it in the third person.

Plan

1 Draw a picture or paste a photo from the video game you are reviewing here.

2 Name of the game: ______________________________

3 The age group it is suitable for: ______________________________

4 What the game can be played on: ______________________________

5 Anything else required to play the game: ______________________________

6 Some benefits of playing the game: ______________________________

____

7 What is the game about? What is the objective? ______________________________

____

____

8 What are some things that happen in the game? List them and how they benefit players.

a ______________________________

b ______________________________

c ______________________________

9 List emotive words and superlatives you can use to convince readers to choose this game.

____

10 Write an opening statement to express the overall opinion of the game and general information about it.

____

____

TARGETING WRITING SKILLS YR 5 © PASCAL PRESS ISBN 9781925726282

Draft

Now you are ready to write a draft of your review of a video game.
Remember to:

- write the name of the game as a heading
- write an opening statement to identify the opinion of the game and use objective language
- write one or more sentences to explain who the game is suitable for and what is required to play it
- write one or more paragraphs to explain what the game is about and how it is played
- use emotive words and superlatives to convince readers to choose the video game
- write a concluding statement to sum up the opinion of the game and link back to the opening statements.

First draft

Write a draft of your review of a video game here.

Feedback

Ask your teacher, classmates or someone at home to suggest what you could do to improve your review.

Revised draft

Self-evaluation

I wrote
- ☐ the name of the game as a heading.
- ☐ an opening statement to identify the opinion of the game.
- ☐ in objective rather than subjective language.
- ☐ a concluding statement to sum up the opinion and linked it back to the opening statement.

I explained
- ☐ who the game is suitable for and what is required to play it.
- ☐ what the game is about and how to play it.

I used
- ☐ emotive words and superlatives.

RECREATING TEXTS Dramatic play

A play is a narrative that has been written for a dramatic performance.

Purpose: This dramatic play entertains with an amusing story about a practical joke and a joker who wasn't so amused.

Audience: The intended audience of this dramatic play is children.

Context: This play is part of a longer story. Stories like this would be found in anthologies and magazines for children, in books of plays or as a chapter of a longer story.

Who's Joking?

Characters: Hannah, Josh

ACT 1

SCENE 1 (*At the bus stop. Hannah is already there. Josh enters.*)

Source: Adapted from *Assignment Fiasco*, Lisa Thompson, Blake Education.

HANNAH: What are you doing here? I thought you changed schools! I was looking forward to a peaceful Josh-free term!

JOSH: Peaceful? Who wants peace? I'm happy to see you too, Hannah. I've even brought you something. (*Josh takes a plastic spider out of his pocket and shoves it at Hannah.*)

HANNAH: AHHHHHHHHH!

JOSH: (*laughing*) I love it! You'd scream at anything. Look — it's not even real. Someone like you should be able to see that. You're such a lung horn!

HANNAH: How many times do I have to tell you? Don't call me that!

JOSH: Call you what? Lung Horn?

HANNAH: Look, Super Pain, just keep your dumb pranks away from me! (*The bus arrives. Hannah moves towards the bus.*) I guess that snake over there is just one of your plastic jokes too.

JOSH: AHHHHHHHHHH! (*Josh pushes past Hannah to get on the bus first.*)

As with other narratives, the play has an orientation that introduces the setting and the characters. It has a series of events, including a complication and a resolution.

1 Orientation: Complete these details about the story.

a Who is the story about? ______

b Where does the story take place? ______

c When does the story take place? ______

2 List the events in order. Circle the complication.

a ______

b ______

c ______

d ______

3 Resolution: How did the story end?

______

 TARGETING WRITING SKILLS YR 5 © PASCAL PRESS ISBN 9781925726282

Change the point of view

In the play, we know what is happening from the characters' words and the stage directions. Rewrite the play as a story with a first-person narrator. Choose to tell the story either from Hannah's or Josh's point of view. You may need to change the title to suit the point of view. You will be able to keep some of the direct speech in your text, but you may not want to keep it all. Depending on the point of view you choose, some of the direct speech will be either 'Hannah said' or 'she said', or 'Josh said' or 'he said'. The rest will be 'I said'.

Remember to:

- write the title of the story first
- begin with the orientation that tells who, when and where, and start it on a new line
- write the story events including the problem or complication
- use direct speech to report words spoken by the characters, and begin a new paragraph for each speaker
- write a resolution to the story to show how the story concludes
- use past tense
- use capital letters for the names of characters.

First draft

Write a draft of your narrative here.

Feedback

Ask your teacher, classmates or someone at home to suggest what you could do to improve your narrative.

Revised draft

Self-evaluation

I wrote ☐ the title on the first line.
☐ the orientation to tell who, when and where.
☐ story events including a problem or complication.
☐ a resolution.
I started ☐ a new paragraph for each speaker.

I used ☐ direct speech to report the actual words spoken by characters.
☐ past tense.
☐ capital letters for the names of characters.

REVIEW

COMPLEX SENTENCES

A **complex sentence** has two or more clauses, including a main clause and one or more independent clauses. Subordinate clauses are linked to the principal clause by a conjunction or a relative pronoun.

Read these complex sentences. In each sentence, highlight the subordinating conjunction, circle the verbs in each clause, underline the main clause in green and underline the subordinate clause in red.

Example: We can't go home until the storm has passed.

a Josh raced to the school bus because there was a snake on the ground.
b The telescope won't work if the glasses are not at the right distance.
c There is no solar eclipse unless the Moon is between the Sun and the Earth.
d The children can't play Minecraft until they finish their homework.
e Whenever it rained a lot, the oval was always wet and slippery.

Add subordinate clauses to give more details about these simple sentences. Use one of these conjunctions: because, if, unless, until, whenever.

a The children couldn't watch TV ______________________________.
b The toaster won't work ______________________________.
c ______________________________ it always rains.
d You must keep the button pressed ______________________________.
e You may see a shooting star ______________________________.
f The accountant took his laptop home ______________________________.

INFORMATIVE TEXT – Procedure

A procedure gives instructions or explains how to do something. Procedures usually have an introductory statement to explain the goal or objective, a list of materials required and a series of numbered steps to follow. This procedure explains how to make a balloon rocket.

Make a Balloon Rocket

Blow up a balloon and see it rocket across the room.

What you do

1. Tie one end of the string to a chair.
2. Thread the other end of the string through a straw.
3. Tie the string to another chair and pull it tight.
4. Blow up the balloon and pinch it, but don't tie it, so the air doesn't escape.
5. Tape the balloon to the straw.
6. Let the balloon go. Watch it fly across the room from one chair to the other.

Did you notice that the list of materials is missing from the procedure?

3

a Underline the materials that are mentioned in the procedure.
b List the materials that are required to make the balloon rocket. Remember to use bullet points.

____

____

____

____

 TARGETING WRITING SKILLS YR 5 © PASCAL PRESS ISBN 9781925726282

IMAGINATIVE TEXT – Dramatic play

A play is a narrative that has been written for a dramatic performance.

4 Rewrite this story as a play. Remember to use capital letters for the names of the characters. Start a new line when each character speaks. Write stage directions in italics.

The Talking Dog

One day a man walked into a restaurant with his dog. The waiter told him that dogs weren't allowed in the restaurant, so he'd have to leave.

The man said that his dog was a talking dog. The waiter was surprised. He told the man that he'd give them both a free meal if the dog could talk.

The man said to the dog, "What is above us in this restaurant?"

"Rrroof!" barked the dog.

The waiter said, "Who is the greatest cricketer who ever lived?"

"Rrroof!" barked the dog.

The waiter told them to leave the restaurant.

Outside, the dog said, "Would it have made a difference if I'd said Donald Bradman?"

Source: *The Talking Dog*, Grammar with a Grin, Peter Clutterbuck, Blake Education.

____

____

____

____

____

____

____

____

____

____

PERSUASIVE TEXT – Review of a video game

The purpose of a video game review is to summarise what happens in the game and present an objective opinion about it.

5 Choose a video game you enjoy (not the one you wrote about in Unit 23).

a Name of the game: ______________________________

b The age group it is suitable for: ______________________________

c What the game can be played on: ______________________________

d Anything else required to play the game: ______________________________

e The objective of the game: ______________________________

f What you like about playing the game: ______________________________

____

g Write a statement from an objective point of view to explain what is good about the game.

____

____

____

GRAMMAR Complex sentences

A complex sentence is constructed from two or more clauses. The clauses make connections between ideas.

One clause tells the main idea. It is called the **main clause** or the **principal clause**. It makes sense on its own.

A **subordinate** or **dependent clause** gives more information about the main idea. It may not make sense on its own.

Subordinate clauses are linked to the principal clause by a conjunction or a relative pronoun.

Conjunctions often used to join subordinate clauses:

after	as	although	unless	before	though
because	whilst	if	once	when	where
so	since	whenever	while	wherever	until

Relative pronouns:

who	whom	whose	which	that

The conjunction or relative pronoun is at the beginning of the subordinate clause. A subordinate clause can occur at the beginning, the end or in the middle of a sentence. When it is in the middle of a sentence, it is called an **embedded clause**.

Example: *The genie, who appeared out of the teapot, granted three wishes.*

The relative pronouns **who** and **whom** are used when talking about people.

The relative pronouns **which** and **that** are used when talking about animals and things.

Examples: *Ryan gave the teapot to his grandmother who liked gold things.*

The teapot, which Ryan bought at the car boot sale, was home to a genie.

The possessive **whose** is used for people, animals and things.

Examples: *The boy, whose telescope was left on the bus, had to phone the bus company.*

The cat, whose paw was hurt, was taken to the vet.

Subordinate clauses that begin with a relative pronoun are adjectival clauses.

They do the work of adjectives and give more information about nouns. They always follow the noun they describe.

In these complex sentences, circle the relative pronoun, underline the adjectival clause and highlight the noun that the clause describes.

Example: The train, which just arrived in the station, is going express to the city.

- **a** The teacher, who is standing over there, is also the soccer coach.
- **b** I bought my telescope at the shop that is on the corner.
- **c** I gave my teapot to my grandmother whom you met yesterday.
- **d** The movie, which we watched last night, was very funny.
- **e** This plumber, whose quote was the cheapest, got the job.

Add adjectival clauses to these main clauses to make complex sentences. Use a relative pronoun to begin the clause. Remember, the clauses always follow the noun they describe.

a The elephant has a new baby calf.

____

b The athlete won a gold medal.

____

c I returned the book to the library.

____

d We bought a new video game at the video store.

____

TARGETING WRITING SKILLS YR 5 © PASCAL PRESS ISBN 9781925726282

Many subordinate clauses do the work of adverbs. They give more information about the verbs and are called adverbial clauses. They are joined to the principal clause using a conjunction and tell us how, when, where, why or for how long things happen.
Example: *The athlete won a gold medal because she had trained very hard.*

In these complex sentences, circle the conjunction, underline the adverbial clause and highlight the verb about which the clause gives more information.
Example: The man arrived at the station after the train had left.

a Although we had it fixed, the toaster still didn't work.
b The genie came out of the teapot whenever Ryan made a wish.
c The pianist practised every day so she would get better and better.

Complex sentences have one main clause and one or more subordinate clauses. The subordinate clauses may be adjectival clauses and give more information about a noun, or they may be adverbial clauses and give more information about a verb. **Some complex sentences have one or more adjectival clauses and one or more adverbial clauses.**
Example: *The athlete, who is standing on the podium, won a gold medal because she trained very hard.*
The principal clause is: *The athlete won a gold medal.*
The adjectival clause tells which athlete: *who is standing on the podium.*
The adverbial clause tells why she won: *because she trained very hard.*

In these complex sentences, highlight the principal clause, underline each subordinate clause in a different colour, and circle the conjunction or relative pronoun that links the clauses.
Example: The athlete, who is standing on the podium, won a gold medal because she trained very hard.

a Although we had it fixed, the toaster that we bought yesterday still didn't work.
b The genie, who was as big as a giant, came out of the teapot whenever Ryan made a wish.
c The telescopes, which we made in class, were great because we could see the moon through them.

When composing text, writers often use a combination of simple, compound and complex sentences, and vary sentence beginnings to make the text flow and add interest.

Read the following text. Put brackets [ ] around the complex sentences. Highlight the principal clauses. Underline the subordinate clauses, using a different colour for adjectival and adverbial clauses. Circle the conjunction or relative pronoun that links the clauses. Hint: The number of verbs in each sentence tells you the number of clauses.

Convict Life

Convicts who were sent to Australia were expected to work hard. When they first arrived, they had to bring supplies with them. By the early 1800s, a lot of the food that the settlers ate was grown in Australia. If the convicts were badly behaved, they could be punished. If they continued to misbehave, they could be sent to a penal colony such as Norfolk Island or Port Arthur. If they behaved well, prisoners who were sentenced to seven years transportation were granted a Ticket of Leave, which allowed them to work for themselves.

INFORMATIVE TEXTS Biography

The purpose of a biography is to give a recount of a person's life written by someone else.

Purpose: This biography recounts details about Bungaree, the first Australian to circumnavigate the continent.

Audience: The intended audience of this biography is children who are learning about the history of Australia and people who made a positive impact on modern day Australia.

Context: Texts like this would be found in history books, magazines and online.

Biographies often include photographs or illustrations.

The title names the person the biography is about.

Bungaree

The orientation introduces the person and provides a brief summary of why their life was important.

Bungaree, a Kuringgai man from the Broken Bay area in New South Wales, was the first Australian to circumnavigate Australia. He was born in about 1775 and moved to Sydney in the 1790s. He learned to speak English quickly and became well-known and liked in the area.

From 1801 to 1803, Bungaree sailed around Australia with Matthew Flinders, a British explorer. This was the first time anyone had sailed all around Australia. It proved that Australia was an island. It also made Bungaree the first Australian-born person to circumnavigate Australia.

A series of paragraphs recounts details of the person's life in order.

Bungaree helped keep the explorers safe. Although he didn't speak the same languages as the Indigenous Australian peoples who lived where they went ashore, Bungaree could communicate with them. He could also tell the explorers what plants were safe to eat and which to avoid.

A concluding paragraph sums up the person's life and what they will be remembered for.

Bungaree went on many other expeditions that explored Australia. He was the first Indigenous Australian person to receive a grant of land from the Governor. He died in Sydney in 1830 and is buried at Rose Bay.

Parts of Speech

Topic-related nouns and noun groups
- first Australian
- Australia
- area
- person
- explorers

Proper nouns
- Bungaree
- Broken Bay
- Australia
- Sydney
- Matthew Flinders

Proper adjectives
- Kuringgai
- Australian
- British
- Indigenous

Past tense
- was
- moved
- learned
- sailed
- proved

Adverbial phrases
- in the 1790s
- in the area
- from 1801 to 1803
- around Australia

Source: https://www.abc.net.au/news/2019-01-25/bungaree-australian-circumnavigate-country-matthew-flinders/10749476
https://australian.museum/about/history/exhibitions/trailblazers/bungaree/

Structure of a biography

Title
The title of a biography names the person who the biography is about.

Circle the title of the biography.

Orientation
The orientation introduces the person and provides a brief summary of why their life was important or remarkable.

Highlight the statement that tells what was important or remarkable about Bungaree's life.

A series of paragraphs
Each paragraph recounts events from Bungaree's life in order.

Underline the statements that tell about events in Bungaree's life. Write notes about the years and the events.

a ______________________________

b ______________________________

c ______________________________

d ______________________________

Concluding paragraph
A concluding paragraph sums up the person's life and what they will be remembered for. If the person has passed, it will tell when they died. If they are still living, it will tell what they may do in the future.

What are the things for which Bungaree will be most remembered?

a ______________________________

b ______________________________

Language features of a biography

Proper nouns
Proper nouns are the special names of people, places, objects and events. Proper nouns always begin with a capital letter. Example: *Bungaree*

Circle all the proper nouns in the text.

Proper adjectives
Proper adjectives are adjectives made from proper nouns. Example: *Australian*

Use a different colour to circle all the proper adjectives in the text.

Adverbial phrases
Adverbial phrases provide more information about how, when, where, why or for how long things happen. They are used to sequence and link events over time. Example: *in the 1790s*

Use a different colour to highlight the adverbial phrases that tell how, when, where, why or for how long things happened in the text.

UNIT 27 FOCUS ON INFORMATIVE TEXTS Writing a biography

Use these notes to write a biography of Ash Barty.

Ash Barty

- born 24 April 1996 in Ipswich, Queensland
- age 4 – began playing tennis and coach saw potential
- age 12 – learned great-grandmother was part of the Ngaragu people from NSW and Victoria
- age 15 – grand slam debut – youngest player in the 2012 Australian Open Competition
- teenage years – Grand Slam title at Wimbledon, ranked World's Junior No. 2
- break from tennis 2014 to 2016 – played cricket with Brisbane Heat
- 2019 – ranked No. 1 in world singles by Women's Tennis Association for 121 weeks
- 2022 – retired from tennis after winning the Australian Open

Plan

1 **Write the title for your biography.** ______________________

2 **Write an orientation that introduces the person and provides a brief summary of why their life (so far) was important or remarkable.**

____

____

3 **Write some of the adverbial phrases you will use to provide information about how, when, where, why or for how long things happened in Ash Barty's tennis career.**

a ______________________

b ______________________

c ______________________

d ______________________

4 **Write sentences to record the most important events in Ash Barty's tennis career prior to 2022.**

a ______________________

____

b ______________________

____

c ______________________

____

d ______________________

____

5 **Write a concluding paragraph to sum up the importance of Ash Barty's tennis career and what she will be remembered for.**

____

____

____

____

Draft

Now you are ready to write a biography of Ash Barty and her tennis career until 2022.

Remember to:

- write your title first, the name of the person
- write an orientation to introduce the person and explain what is important or remarkable about their life
- write a series of paragraphs that recounts events in order
- write a concluding paragraph that sums up the importance of the person's career
- use past tense
- use capital letters for proper nouns and proper adjectives
- write in sentences with capital letters and full stops.

First draft

Write a draft of your biography here.

Feedback

Ask your teacher, classmates or someone at home to suggest what you could do to improve your biography.

Revised draft

Self-evaluation

I wrote ☐ the title on the first line.
☐ an orientation to introduce the person.
☐ a series of paragraphs to record events in order.
☐ a concluding paragraph to sum up the importance of the person's career.
☐ in present tense.
☐ in sentences with capital letters and full stops.

I used ☐ capital letters for proper nouns and proper adjectives.

IMAGINATIVE TEXTS Shape poems

The purpose of poetry is to help us understand and appreciate the world around us. Shape poems, sometimes called concrete poems, add a visual element to the words. The words are written in the shape of what is written about. Shape poems can be written either around the outline, or inside the outline, to create a picture.

Purpose: These shape poems present a new way of looking at natural or manufactured objects in the environment.

Audience: The intended audience of these shape poems is children.

Context: Poems like these are often included in anthologies and magazines for children.

Poems:

- do not usually have sentences that follow the normal structure, beginning with a capital letter and ending with a full stop like other texts do
- are usually written in verse which means they follow a set rhythm and often include rhyme
- are usually arranged in stanzas, or groups of lines, that begin with a capital letter and end with a full stop. Each line of the stanza also begins with a capital letter whether it is a new sentence or not.

Shape/concrete poems:

- may have features similar to other poems but are arranged to also have a visual effect
- have lines that may wrap around each other without an obvious start or finish, other than the capital letter, in order to create the visual effect.

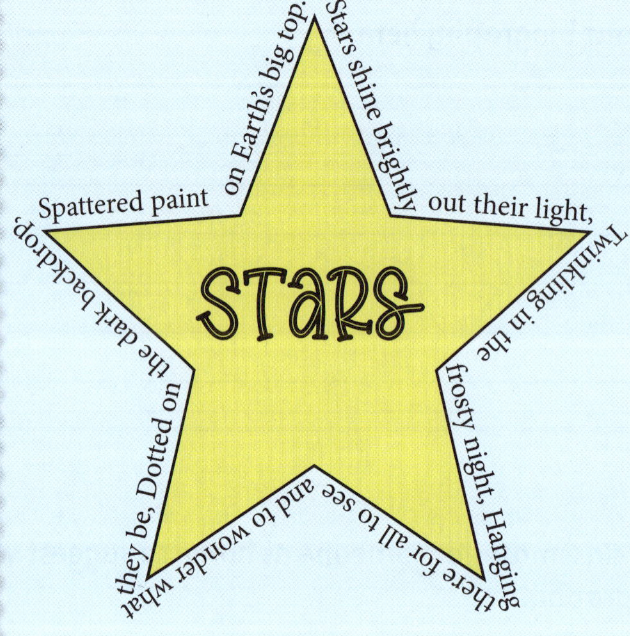

Umbrella

When white clouds
dance across the sky,
You keep me where I'm safe and dry.
But when the dark clouds gather round
Making their obnoxious sound,
You take me out and hold me high
So I get wet, and you stay dry.
And when the storm clouds roll away,
You shake me out, put me away.
I really wish you'd let me stay
And play with you on a sunny day.

Language features of poetry

Rhyming words

- light/night
- see/be
- backdrop/top
- sky/dry
- round/sound
- high/dry
- away/stay/play/day

Personification

- the umbrella
- clouds dance

Metaphors

- spattered paint
- Earth's big top

Repetition

- you keep me/you take me/and hold me/you shake me/put me

TARGETING WRITING SKILLS YR 5 © PASCAL PRESS ISBN 9781925726282

Structure of a shape poem

Title

A poem usually has a title that tells you what the poem is about. The shape of the poem may also indicate what the poem is about with or without a title.

Only one of these poems has a title. Write a suitable title for each.

a ______________________________

b ______________________________

Verse

Poems are often written in verse and usually have a rhythm that is different from normal written text or speech. Each line of verse begins with a capital letter whether it is the beginning of a new sentence or not. However, not all lines will end with a full stop. In a shape poem, the lines are not always easy to see, but a capital letter will often show the beginning of a new line.

Read the poems.

a Circle the capital letters that would begin a line of verse if the poem was written in straight verse, rather than a shape.

b Underline the last word of each line.

c Use brackets [ ] to show where each line of verse begins and ends.

d Write the first two lines of the star poem here.

____

e Write the last two lines of the umbrella poem here.

____

Language features of poems

Rhyme

Rhyme is a feature common to many but not all poems. These two shape poems rhyme. The rhyming words occur at the ends of lines.

a Use different colours to circle the pairs of words that rhyme.

b Write the pairs of words that rhyme here.

____

____

Personification

The umbrella poem is written in the first person from the umbrella's point of view, as if the umbrella was a person. Sometimes other animals and objects are described as if they are people, for example, 'white clouds dance', 'dark clouds gather'.

Highlight the examples of personification in the poem.

Metaphors

Similes and metaphors are similar. Both are ways of describing things. A **simile** says that something *is like* something else. A **metaphor** says that something *is* something else. For example, in the star poem, the poet says that stars are 'spattered paint' and that the sky is 'Earth's big top'.

a Write another metaphor to describe stars.

____

b Write a metaphor to describe an umbrella.

____

TERM FOUR

UNIT 29

FOCUS ON

IMAGINATIVE TEXTS

Writing a shape poem

Write a poem about an object, either natural or manufactured. It is best to choose an object that has a distinct shape. Write your poem first, then decide if you will write it around the outline like the star poem, or inside the shape like the umbrella poem. Choose your own object, or start with one of these suggestions: UFO, rocket ship, donut, teardrop, a cup, the moon, a bird, Earth.

Plan

1 Draw the outline of your object here. Make it as large as possible so you have plenty of room for writing your poem.

2 **Title**
What is the title of your poem? What object will your poem be about?

____

3 **Features of the object**
List features of the object, including what it looks like, how it moves, what is special about it, and perhaps your reasons for choosing it.

____
____
____

4 **Describe the object**
List adjectives that could be used to describe the object. Write suitable similes and metaphors too.

____
____
____

5 **Rhyming words**
Choose some of the features or adjectives and list rhyming words to use in your poem.

____
____
____

TARGETING WRITING SKILLS YR 5 © PASCAL PRESS ISBN 9781925726282

Draft

Now you are ready to write a draft of your shape poem. You will write the poem as verse first and only write it in or around the shape when you have the words right. Keep your poem short, about 6–10 lines is best at first.

Remember to:

- write the title of the poem first
- begin each new line with a capital letter
- include rhymes at the end of lines
- use examples of personification, similes or metaphors
- decide if you will write the poem in or around the outline of the object.

First draft

Write a draft of your poem here.

Now that you have the words of your poem how you want them, write them in or around the shape on the previous page.

Feedback

Ask your teacher, classmates or someone at home to suggest what you could do to improve your poem.

Revised draft

Self-evaluation

I used ☐ rhyming words at the end of lines.
☐ personification.
☐ a simile.
☐ a metaphor.

I wrote ☐ the title on the first line.
I began ☐ each new line with a capital letter.

PERSUASIVE TEXTS Discussion

The purpose of a discussion is to present different points of view about an issue. It allows the reader to think about different points of view before making an informed decision.

Purpose: This discussion presents different points of view about compulsory voting.

Audience: The intended audience of this discussion is people who are considering whether voting should be compulsory or not.

Context: Discussions like this can be informal conversations or interviews for radio or television.

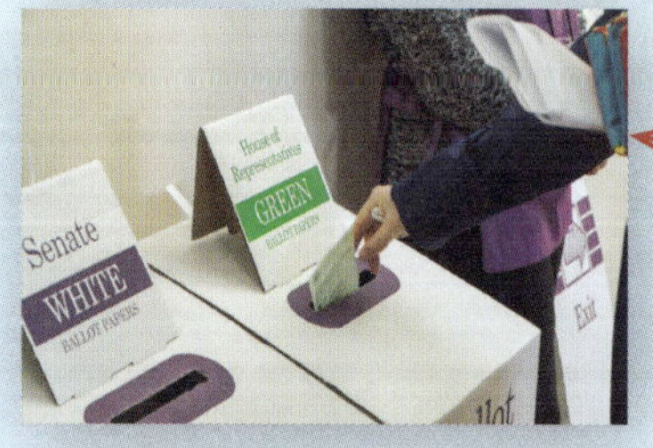

A discussion may be accompanied by a photograph or illustration, or video.

A title identifies the topic or issue. It may be in the form of a question.

Should Voting be Compulsory?

Opening statements introduce the topic and present both sides of the issue or points of view (P).

Frankie: Voting should be compulsory. It is a responsibility of everyone in a democratic society.

Alex: Surely people living in a democracy should be able to choose.

A series of paragraphs gives arguments for and against the topic. They provide evidence (E) and explain (E) reasons for holding the point of view.

Frankie: People still have choices. They can leave the ballot paper blank or spoil it in some way. Or pay the $20 fine. When voting is compulsory, the winner really does win most votes and the support of most people. That doesn't happen when voting is voluntary.

Alex: But some might just vote for anyone, especially someone with an expensive ad campaign. And voting for someone you don't even like, just because you have to, doesn't make sense.

A conclusion sums up the discussion and gives a recommendation. It links (L) back to the opening statements.

Frankie: People will be better informed and make better choices if they have to vote. Candidates will have to think about everyone in their electorate, not just the wealthy or vocal ones.

Alex: Even when voting is voluntary, people can still make their voices heard. Whether compulsory or not, candidates should do a lot more to benefit those voting for them.

Parts of Speech

Topic-related nouns and noun-groups
- voting
- democratic society
- democracy
- choice
- votes

Present tense
- is
- have
- can
- does
- vote

Evaluative language
- should
- responsibility
- choose
- really
- most
- just because

Connectives
- or
- when
- but
- if
- whether

Source: State Library of New South Wales *Compulsory Voting — For and Against* https://legalanswers.sl.nsw.gov.au/hot-topics-voting-and-elections/compulsory-voting-and-against

TARGETING WRITING SKILLS YR 5 © PASCAL PRESS ISBN 9781925726282

Structure of a discussion

PEEL

A discussion presents different points of view about an issue to allow the reader to think before making an informed decision. It may be written using what is known as the PEEL structure. Sometimes a writer presents both points of view in an article. In this discussion, each speaker presents their own point of view on the topic. The discussion presents the words actually spoken by each person.

Title

The title identifies the topic or issue to be discussed. Each main word of the title is capitalised. It may take the form of a question.

Circle the title.

Opening statements

The opening statements introduce the topic and present both sides of the topic so the reader understands the points of view (P) being discussed. Each speaker in this discussion presents a different point of view.

Use a different colour for each speaker to highlight the statements in which they introduce their point of view.

Arguments

A series of arguments provides evidence (E) and explains (E) reasons for the writer's point of view. They link back to the point of view expressed in the opening statements.

a Highlight the main ideas that each speaker uses to provide evidence and explain reasons for their point of view.

b Frankie is for compulsory voting. Alex is against compulsory voting. In a few words, write their three main reasons for holding that point of view.

Frankie: ______________________________

Alex: ______________________________

Conclusion and recommendation

The conclusion and recommendation link back (L) to the opening statements.

Underline the words that link back to the opening statements.

Circle the recommendation.

Now that you have heard both points of view, you can decide on your own point of view. Write it here.

(P) ______________________________

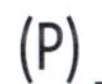

Language features of a discussion

Evaluative language

In the arguments for and against compulsory voting, each speaker puts forward their point of view using strong evaluative language to convince others to agree with them.

Write the words each speaker uses to influence your opinion about compulsory voting.

____

List other strong words that could be used to convince readers of an opinion.

____

PERSUASIVE TEXTS

Writing a discussion

It is almost time to decide on a new school captain for the next school year. You decide to stand as a candidate.

Write a discussion that takes place when you are interviewed by someone who doesn't agree with your views. You need to convince the student body to vote for you. Set the discussion out as an interview with the exact words each speaker says, as in the discussion on page 66.

Plan

1 **Think of three things that you most want to achieve in your role as school captain. Write them and the reasons for wanting to achieve them on the lines.**

As school captain, I want to ...

a ______________________ because ______________________

____

b ______________________ because ______________________

____

c ______________________ because ______________________

____

2 **Now think of reasons others may have for arguing against those goals. List them.**

a ______________________ because ______________________

____

b ______________________ because ______________________

____

c ______________________ because ______________________

____

3 **List evaluative words you could use to convince students to vote for you.**

____

4 **List evaluative words the interviewer could use to convince students to not vote for you.**

____

5 **Write a statement to introduce your point of view.**

____

6 **Write a concluding statement to sum up your point of view and tell students (recommend) why they should vote for you.** ______________________

____

7 **Write a title to introduce your discussion.**

____

 TARGETING WRITING SKILLS YR 5 © PASCAL PRESS ISBN 9781925726282

Draft

Now you are ready to write a draft of the discussion that takes place between you and the person interviewing you about your school captain candidacy. Remember to set it out like the discussion on page 66.

Remember to:

- write the title first to identify the topic
- write an opening statement in which the interviewer introduces you
- write an opening statement in which you introduce your main idea (P)
- write paragraphs that present evidence (E) for and explain (E) each point of view
- write a conclusion that includes a recommendation and links (L) back to the opening statement
- use evaluative language to convince readers of your recommendation
- use capital letters at the beginning of sentences and full stops at the end.

First draft

Write a draft of your discussion here.

Feedback

Ask your teacher, classmates or someone at home to suggest what you could do to improve your discussion.

Revised draft

Self-evaluation

I wrote ☐ the title to identify the topic.
☐ an opening statement to introduce my point of view (P).
☐ paragraphs with evidence (E) and explanations (E) to support the points of view.
☐ a conclusion that included a recommendation and linked back to the opening statement (L).

I set ☐ it out like an interview, recording the words spoken by each speaker.

I used ☐ evaluative language.

RECREATING TEXTS Persuasive text – Discussion

The purpose of a discussion is to present different points of view about an issue. It allows the reader to think about different points of view before making an informed decision.

Purpose: This discussion presents different points of view about the state of medical care and ambulance services available in a small community.

Audience: The intended audience of this discussion is people who are interested in the state of medical care and ambulance services available in their community.

Context: Discussions like this may be reported in local newspapers or in news reports on radio or television.

You are a news reporter. A group of unhappy constituents recently visited the office of a newly elected Member of Parliament to request better medical care and a reliable ambulance service in their town. Read their point of view. Consider how the Member of Parliament might respond to it. Write an article that discusses both points of view.

We have lived in Lowtown for a long time. For all those years, we have never had a good reliable ambulance service. It is about time we did. Many people need access to medical treatment and are not getting it. Sometimes the ambulances take hours to come. Sometimes they come too late, and sometimes they don't come at all. It is just not good enough.

For years, the government has ignored our community. You must change this. We want to have our voices heard and our needs met. We pay taxes too. We need good medical care, just like everybody else. A reliable 24-hour ambulance service is part of that care.

What will you do to make sure a reliable ambulance service is built in Lowtown? If you can't do this, then you are not representing all the people of your district.

Plan

1. **Highlight what the people of Lowtown are requesting and the arguments supporting their request.**
2. **Consider how the Member of Parliament (MP) may respond to their request and arguments. The MP may or may not agree with some or all of the request.**

   ____

   ____

   ____

3. **As a news reporter, write a concluding statement that sums up the arguments.**

   ____

4. **Write a recommendation.** ______________________________

   ____

TARGETING WRITING SKILLS YR 5 © PASCAL PRESS ISBN 9781925726282

Write an article discussing two points of view

You have read two opinions of the people of Lowtown, and you have considered the opinions of the Member of Parliament. You have also written a recommendation from your own point of view as a news reporter.

Now you will write an article for your newspaper that discusses both points of view.

Remember to:

- write a title (headline) to identify the topic
- write opening statements to introduce both points of view (P)
- write short paragraphs to present arguments with evidence (E) and explanations (E) from both points of view
- write a concluding statement to sum up the points of view, linking back to the opening statement (L)
- write a recommendation from your point of view
- use emotive words and evaluative language
- use capital letters at the beginning of sentences and full stops at the end.

First draft

Write a draft of your discussion here.

Feedback

Ask your teacher, classmates or someone at home to suggest what you could do to improve your discussion.

Revised draft

Self-evaluation

I wrote ☐ the title to identify the topic.
☐ an opening statement to introduce my point of view (P).
☐ short paragraphs to provide evidence (E) and explanations (E) from both viewpoints.
☐ a concluding statement that links to the opening statements (L).
☐ a recommendation.

I used ☐ emotive words and evaluative language.
☐ capital letters and full stops in sentences.

TERM 4

REVIEW

COMPLEX SENTENCES

A **complex sentence** is constructed from two or more clauses. One is a **main clause** or **principal clause** which makes sense on its own. The others are **subordinate** or **dependent clauses** that give more information about the main idea and are linked to the principal clause by a conjunction or a relative pronoun. The conjunction or relative pronoun is at the beginning of the subordinate clause. Subordinate clauses can occur at the beginning, the end or in the middle of a sentence.

In these complex sentences, highlight the principal clause, underline each subordinate clause in a different colour, and circle the conjunction or relative pronoun that links the clauses.

Example: The athlete, who is standing on the podium, won a gold medal because she trained very hard.

- **a** Although he didn't speak the same languages as the Indigenous Australian peoples who lived where they went ashore, Bungaree could communicate with them.
- **b** Poems do not usually have sentences that follow the normal structure.
- **c** Each line of a stanza begins with a capital letter whether it is a new sentence or not.
- **d** Write a discussion that takes place when you are interviewed by someone who doesn't agree with your views.
- **e** It is important to eat nutritious food that is available everywhere so you stay healthy.
- **f** My mother, who is a doctor, had to work on the weekend because a lot of other doctors were sick with Covid.
- **g** Synthetic materials, which are made by people, are used to make many different products.
- **h** Astronauts who live on the International Space Station have to zip themselves into sleeping bags so they don't float out of the bags when they are asleep.

INFORMATIVE TEXT – Biography

A biography recounts details of a person's life. It is written by someone else.

Use these notes to write a biography of Linda Burney, Indigenous Australian teacher and politician.

- 2022 – first Indigenous Australian woman to be Minister for Indigenous Australians in Australian Parliament
- 1957 – born in Whitton, New South Wales
- 2003 – first Indigenous Australian person in NSW Parliament
- 2016 – first Indigenous Australian woman elected to Australian House of Representatives
- 1978 – first Indigenous Australian graduate from Mitchell College of Advanced Education (now called Charles Sturt University) – Diploma of Teaching and a PhD
- raised by a great-aunt and uncle, poor family
- member of the Wiradjuri Nation
- committed to Aboriginal rights in education, reconciliation and politics

TARGETING WRITING SKILLS YR 5 © PASCAL PRESS ISBN 9781925726282

IMAGINATIVE TEXT – Shape poems

Shape poems, sometimes called concrete poems, add a visual element to the words. The words are written in the shape of what is written about. Shape poems can be written either around the outline, or inside the outline, to create the picture.

3 Write a shape poem about an apple.

a What is the title of your poem? ____________________

b List adjectives to describe the apple. Consider:
- colour ____________________
- size and shape ____________________
- taste ____________________
- smell ____________________
- sounds ____________________

c List pairs of rhyming words that you could use in your poem.

____

d Write your poem on the lines first, then write it inside or around the outline of the apple.

____
____
____
____
____
____

PERSUASIVE TEXT – Discussion

The purpose of a discussion is to present different points of view about an issue.

A group of Year 5 children were discussing how they should celebrate the end of the school year. These are some of the things they thought about:
Should we celebrate at school or have an excursion? How much will the celebrations cost? Can everyone afford the celebration? What if some can't afford it?

4 a List suggestions with reasons for having a celebration at school.

____
____
____

b List suggestions with reasons for having an excursion to celebrate.

____
____
____

c Write a discussion that presents both sides of the topic. Write a concluding statement with a recommendation.

____
____
____
____
____
____

ANSWERS

Answers are not provided where students are asked to write their own texts.

TERM ONE

Unit 1

Page 2

1 **a** Q **b** S **c** S **d** E **e** E **f** Q **g** E **h** C

2 Answers will vary but must be written as the correct type of sentence.

Page 3

- **a** Did you go to the skate park on the weekend?
- **b** The shopping mall was closed due to the floods.
- **c** Why did you do that?
- **d** Hooray!

4 Stop! Why are you here? You are not allowed in here. Didn't you see the sign? The sign says no one must enter. Leave now!

5 Answers will vary. Examples:

- **a** The big brown dog chased the boy with the green cap.
- **b** The little girl caught a fish as big as her.
- **c** The gardener with the floppy hat trimmed the unruly hedge.
- **d** The happy customer bought a huge birthday cake.

6 I live on an apple farm just outside Stanthorpe. We grow juicy, delicious Red Gala apples.

Unit 2

Page 5

1-4 How Do Bicycle Reflectors Work?

Most bicycles have reflectors at the back, at the front and on the wheels. The purpose of the reflectors is to help keep the cyclists safe when riding at night. The reflectors warn other road users that the cyclist is there. But how do they work?

When light hits an object, it can go through it (transmit), bounce off (reflect) or be stopped (absorbed). A bicycle reflector is made to reflect light straight back to the light source.

Reflectors are usually made from transparent plastic. The outside surface is very smooth. This allows light (such as from a car's headlights or from a torch) to enter the reflector.

The back of the reflector is made up of lots of angled prisms. When the light enters the reflector, it hits the prisms. The prisms reflect the light back out in the direction it came from.

When the person who is close to the light source, such as the driver of a vehicle, sees the reflected light, they know that the cyclist is there.

3

- **a** reflectors reflect light back to the source
- **b** light enters through transparent plastic
- **c** prisms reflect the light back
- **d** drivers see reflected light and know a cyclist is there

5

- **a** Reflectors help to keep cyclists safe.
- **b** Motorists see the reflected light.
- **c** Light hits the prisms.

6 Answers will vary. Examples:

- **a** Transmit means that an object allows light to go through it.
- **b** Reflect means that the light bounces back off an object.
- **c** Absorbed means that the object stops the light going any further.

Unit 3

Page 6

2-4 Answers will vary. Examples:

Rainbows

- multicoloured arc in the sky
- made by refraction and reflection in certain conditions
- early morning or late afternoon when sun is low in sky
- sun must be behind you, water droplets in air in front of you
- sunlight must strike the water droplets at the right angle
- sunlight appears white – made up of all colours of the spectrum
- every colour has a different wavelength
- when light from the air enters a water droplet, it slows down and bends (refraction)
- reflects off the inside of the droplet – separates into different wavelengths (colours) – reflected at different angles
- speeds up and changes direction again when leaving the water droplet (refraction)
- we see the different colours of the rainbow: red, orange, yellow, green, blue, indigo and violet

1 How are rainbows made?

5 Paragraph 1 conditions required for rainbows to form
Paragraph 2 sunlight refracts (bends) when entering a water droplet
Paragraph 3 sunlight reflects off back of water droplet and separates into different colours
Paragraph 4 we see all the colours of the rainbow

Unit 4

Page 9

1-3 Convict Life

Ann and I entered the tent and Sergeant Scott got straight down to business.

"You have been assigned to look after my family and lodgings," he said. "As well as gathering water, preparing meals and cleaning, you will do anything my wife, Charlotte, requires of you. You will also assist with farming. Any questions?"

We shook our heads.

At first, Ann and I lived in a small tent next to the sergeant's home while a hut was built.

Ann was in charge of cooking while I washed and mended clothes. I washed in a nearby stream and draped clothes over rocks and bushes to dry.

We knew how lucky we were to be working for the sergeant, rather than the harsh work of making bricks or building roads. All convicts worked — that was our punishment and why we were here.

3 tent, lodgings, gathering water, assist with farming, small tent, hut was built, washed in a nearby stream, draped clothes over rocks and bushes to dry, harsh work, making bricks or building roads, convicts, punishment

4 lucky, harsh work, our punishment

5 Ann was in charge of cooking, while Jane washed and mended clothes. Jane washed in a nearby stream and draped clothes over rocks and bushes to dry. They knew how lucky they were to be working for the sergeant.

6 Answers may vary. Example: "We are so lucky to be working for the sergeant," said Jane.

Unit 5

Page 10

Answers will vary. Examples:

1 Life in a Floating Prison

2 No matter our age, we were all crammed together into the damp, dark, rotting hulks until we could be transported to Australia.

3 People were sick and dying. I could hear children and old people crying. Their bellies rumbled with hunger. Most people were not criminals. Like me, they were just poor and hungry. Our clothes were ragged and filthy and smelt bad after weeks without washing.

4 "I am so hungry. Do you think we will ever eat a proper meal again?" said Jane.
"I am so cold," said Ann. "I wish I had that blanket to keep us warm."
"All we wanted was something to eat and something to keep us warm," said Jane. "It's not fair. I hope things are better in Australia."

5 moaned, sat, thought, slept, talked, wriggled, grumbled

6 Life was harsh in the floating prisons, but the prisoners didn't know what awaited them when they were transported to Australia.

Unit 6

Page 13

1-6, 8a

Not All Single-Use Plastic is Bad

We are always being told to stop using single-use plastics because they are bad for the environment. However, sometimes single-use plastics are not only useful, but they are also essential.

It is crucial for health professionals to use single-use plastics to avoid the spread of infection. Scientists must also protect themselves and their materials with single-use plastics. Moreover, plastic packaging is essential to keep food fresh and safe in emergencies, both locally and internationally.

Eco-friendly products are expensive. If people on low incomes had to buy them, then they would have to go without something else, maybe even food.

Single-use plastic products like bendable straws help people with disabilities to live independently. Many also rely on pre-cut food that is often packaged in plastic.

Yes, we can and should reduce our use of single-use plastics. However, we must also remember that there are times when single-use plastic is necessary.

7 a If health professionals couldn't use single-use plastics, then infections would increase.
  b If food couldn't be packaged in plastic, then it couldn't be kept fresh and safe in emergencies.

8 bad, useful, essential, crucial, avoid, must, fresh, safe, emergencies, expensive, go without, independently, rely, can, should, must, necessary

9 Answers will vary. Example: It is crucial for health professionals to use single-use plastics to avoid the spread of infection.

Unit 7

Page 14

Answers will vary. Examples:

1 Screen time for children should be limited.

2 When children spend too much time on their screens, they are not spending enough time on more important things like spending time with family and friends.

3 Answers will vary.

4 When children's screen time is limited, they will sleep better, learn better and even be better behaved.

Unit 8

Page 16

1-3 **The Old Bark School**

(an extract) by Henry Lawson

It was built of bark and poles, and the floor was full of holes
Where each leak in rainy weather made a pool;
And the walls were mostly cracks lined with calico and sacks,
There was little need for windows in the school.

Then we rode to school and back by the rugged gully-track,
On the old grey horse that carried three or four;
And he looked so very wise that he lit the master's eyes
Every time he put his head in at the door.

And we learnt the world in scraps from some ancient dingy maps
Long discarded by the public-schools in town;
And as nearly every book dated back to Captain Cook
Our geography was somewhat upside-down.

4 Answers will vary. Example:
We went to school in a hut made of bark. When it rained, the roof leaked, and the wind whistled in through holes in the walls. Our maps were old and upside-down because they were made for the Northern Hemisphere.

Term 1 Review

Page 18

1 Answers will vary. Examples:
  a (Q) Did the cyclist fit new reflectors to her bike?
  b (C) Fit new reflectors to your bike.
  c (E) New reflectors!

2 Answers will vary. Examples:
  a (Q) Should single-use plastic be banned?
  b (C) Ban single-use plastic.
  c (E) Ban single-use plastic now!

3 Answers will vary. Examples:
  a The new student entered the noisy school room.
  b The lone cyclist rode down the long and winding road.
  c The young farmer saddled her bay horse.
  d The baby humpback whale swam in the warm water.
  e The girl in the purple shirt won the cross-country race.

4 Answers will vary.

Page 19

5-8 Answers will vary.

TERM TWO

Unit 9

Page 20

1 a Very little rain falls in deserts, yet many living things survive there.
  b He missed the bus, so he had to walk to school.
  c The children could choose to watch a movie, or they could go to the beach.
  d Dragons are mythical creatures, and they often appear in fantasy stories.

2 a The old man didn't go out very often, nor did he have many visitors.
  b The girl couldn't ride a skateboard, nor could she ride a bike.
  c Humans don't have wings to fly, nor do they have gills to breathe under water.

3 a yet b nor c and d for e or f so g but

Page 21

4 a P The house at the bottom of the hill is vacant.
  b C The author who visited our class lives in Sydney.
  c A The huge, orange crabs live in the ocean.
  d P The boy in the green shirt came first in the race.

5 Answers will vary. Examples:
  a C The boys, who should be doing their homework, are playing football.
  b P The bird with a sore wing flew onto the tree.
  c C The movie, that we watched last night, was very funny.
  d A The grumpy baby wouldn't stop crying.

6 a cat's tail
  b the neighbour's pet
  c the book's cover
  d Tina's friend
  e the lions' cages
  f the principal's office
  g the teachers' staffroom
  h a giraffe's neck
  i Traz's brother

7

can't	who's	hasn't	we're	should've	don't	here's
has not	do not	here is	can not	who is	we are	should have

Unit 10

Page 23

1-4a, 5

Giant Spider Crabs

Giant Spider Crabs grow up to 16 cm across their shell and 70 cm across their legs. They mostly live alone in ocean waters south of Australia.

However, during winter, huge groups gather in the shallower waters of Port Phillip Bay. The crabs climb on top of each other in piles up to 2 m high and over 100 m long.

Like other crustaceans, Giant Spider Crabs have an exoskeleton, a hard external shell. The exoskeleton doesn't grow as our skin does. The crabs must shed their old shell (moult) to grow bigger.

It takes about an hour for a Giant Spider Crab to moult, but the soft new shell takes several days to harden. The legs are soft too, and walking is not easy. This makes it difficult to escape from predators.

Scientists think the Giant Spider Crabs gather and moult at the same time for safety. The chance of any individual crab being eaten is reduced.

After they have moulted, the Giant Spider Crabs return to deeper water.

3 Answers will vary. Examples:
  a gather together in winter
  b have exoskeleton
  c moult
  d gather for safety

ANSWERS

4 b They mostly live alone in ocean waters south of Australia.
6 they, groups, crustaceans
7 a in ocean waters south of Australia
b on top of each other
c to grow bigger
d about an hour
e during winter
f to deeper water

Unit 12

Page 27

1, 2, 4, 6, 7a

Simpkins Meets the Dragon

Simpkins thought he'd never been so frightened in all his life. And then he heard the slow whup, whup, whup of dragon wings and realised it was always possible to feel more fear. The beast was coming back. Simpkins grabbed a long, knobbly bone in each hand. He tried not to think about whose legs he was holding.

Whup, whup, whooomph. The huge dragon glided into the cave's entrance and began walking along the tunnel to his main lair. Simpkins could hear it snorting. The shuffle of claws on chalk changed to a clanking rattle as the dragon reached its lair. A sudden flare of flame killed any thought Simpkins had of hiding. The cave lit up like his brothers' cottage when all its candles were lit. Simpkins hoisted the bones he was holding in what he hoped was a threatening pose.

The dragon glared at him, a flame still flickering from its nostrils. "You dare to threaten me in my own lair?" it roared. "You humans have no respect!"

3 a Simpkins: frightened, brave, human
b The dragon: wings, huge, glides, snorting, shuffles, claws, breathes fire, doesn't like humans

5 Answers will vary. Example: Simpkins was as scared as if he had just been called to the principal's office.

7 b he'd = he had (C), cave's (P), brother's (P)

Unit 14

Page 31

1-3 a, 4, 5

New! Environmentally-friendly Greenline Skateboards

Need an incentive to get off your screens and outside in the fresh air? A Greenline Skateboard is exactly what you need.

Skateboarding — the healthy alternative — have fun, get fit and reduce your carbon footprint all at the same time.

Needing no battery, using no petrol and made from 100% recycled materials, the new Greenline Skateboards are completely harmless to the environment and safe for skaters of all ages.

Whether you skate alone or with friends; just for thrills or cruising around town, Greenline Skateboards are the perfect choice. We've got a Greenline deck to suit every taste.

Wheels with grip and stability will have you hopping curbs, grinding rails and mastering ollie tricks in no time.

World champion Keegan Falcon says, "I wouldn't trust any other. Greenline's the only skateboard for me."

Get your skates on with a Greenline Skateboard now. Available at all reputable stores where skateboards are sold, on the street and online. Mention this ad for a whopping 25% discount.

3 b healthy, harmless to environment, safe, fun, cruising around town

6 a Skateboarding — the healthy alternative — have fun, get fit and reduce your carbon footprint all at the same time.
b Whether you skate alone or with friends; just for thrills or cruising around town, Greenline Skateboards are the perfect choice.
c Wheels with grip and stability will have you hopping curbs, grinding rails and mastering ollie tricks in no time.

7 Answers will vary. Example: Our shorts are not only a perfect fit they come in every colour of the rainbow to suit your every mood – pastel for the quiet times and fluoro for when you want to pop a party.

Unit 16

Page 34

1 Benefits of healthy takeaway food: save you time, low-fat, low-sugar foods, tasty, healthy, good nutritional value

2-7 Answers will vary.

Term 2 Review

Page 36

1 a but
b yet
c so
d and
e nor
f or
g yet

2 Answers will vary. Examples:
a (A) Giant Spider Crabs live in the deep ocean.
b (A) The fierce dragon entered the dark and gloomy cave.
c (C) The children, who were visiting on holidays, rode their skateboards down the hill.
d (P) This burger with its spicy mustard is the best I've ever tasted.

3 Answers will vary.

Page 37

4 & 5 Answers will vary.

TERM THREE

Unit 17

Page 38

1 a I went to the doctor because I hurt my foot during soccer.
b I got my foot x-rayed so the doctor could see the damage.
c The entire school crammed into the hall because the principal was making an announcement.
d Since it was raining, our excursion was cancelled.
e The bus drivers were on strike, as they wanted safer buses.

Page 39

2 a Unless your scores improve, you won't make it into the team.
b Although they are mythical creatures, dragons are quite beautiful.
c The river will flood again if it doesn't stop raining.
d The students were told to stay home if they were unwell.
e I won't make it to practice on time unless the bus arrives soon.

3 a The children had pizza after the game was over.
b I was feeling excited about the concert before I knew we were going.
c We always go to the park when my cousins come over.
d Whenever we go to the zoo, we always feed the kangaroos first.
e We must do our best until it is the last day of school.

4 Answers will vary. Examples:
a I will make breakfast on Sunday while you walk the dogs.
b We always go to the cinema when a new movie is showing.
c I was late for school although I woke up early.
d This bicycle is the best because it has lots of gears.
e The tablet will not work unless you are connected to the internet.
f My mum drives carefully so she doesn't have an accident.
g The farmer takes the horse to the vet whenever it has a limp.
h The soccer player can't play again until the paramedics assess her.
i The bridge was built over the river since people had to get to the other side.
j The jug was empty after everyone had a drink.

Unit 18

Page 41

1–3 a, 4 a, 5 a

Make a Refracting Telescope

A refracting telescope uses two magnifying glasses to bend light and bring it into focus. For this to work, you need to find the length between two lenses that brings the image into focus. This is called finding the focal length.

Materials

- a long cardboard tube
- 1 magnifying glass, about 1 cm diameter
- 1 magnifying glass, about 3 cm diameter
- scissors
- adhesive tape
- a ruler
- a book with writing

Steps

1 Hold the larger magnifying glass over the writing. Put the smaller magnifying glass between the bigger glass and your eye.
2 Move the smaller magnifying glass closer or further away from the larger glass until the writing is clear. The print will be upside down.
3 Measure the distance between the two glasses. This will be the focal length of your telescope.
4 Tape the magnifying glasses inside the cardboard tube with the focal length between them.
5 Look at the night sky with your refracting telescope.

3 **b** Materials, Steps
4 **b** hold, move, measure, tape, look
5 **b** over, between, from, inside, at
6 Answers will vary. Examples:
  a Kick the ball between the goal posts.
  b Be at school before nine o'clock.
  c Write your name at the top of the paper.
  d Put your book in your bag.

Unit 19

Page 42

1 Answers will vary. Examples:
  a Make a Model of a Solar Eclipse
  b Make a model to explain what happens during a solar eclipse.
2 a globe, a torch, a ball on a string
3 place, hold, turn on, turn, suspend
4 on the table, in front of the globe, between the globe and the torch, in a straight line
5 1 Place the globe on the table.
  2 Place the torch on the table in front of the globe.
  3 Turn the globe until your part of the globe is facing the torch.
  4 Suspend the ball between the globe and the torch so they are in a straight line.
  5 Turn on the torch. Your part of the globe should be in shadow like a solar eclipse.

Unit 20

Page 45

1 & 5

Genie in a Teapot

Characters: Ryan, Pritesh, Stall owner, Genie

ACT 1

SCENE 1	(*at a car boot sale*)
RYAN:	How much have we made?
PRITESH:	(*counts the money*) Twenty-one dollars and fifty cents — that's ten dollars each.
RYAN:	Um, ten dollars and seventy-five cents!
PRITESH:	Time to pack up then.
RYAN:	(*Ryan sees a teapot on another stall.*) Hey, look at that teapot!
PRITESH:	Gross or what!
RYAN:	I know my Nan would love it! She loves gold stuff like that.
RYAN:	(*speaking to the stall owner*) How much is the teapot?
STALL OWNER:	One dollar fifty.
RYAN:	Done! (*pays the stall owner*)
PRITESH:	You've been done mate.
	Later
PRITESH:	What's going on? Everything you wish for is coming true. (*sees smoke coming from the teapot*) And look! What's happening to your teapot?
GENIE:	(*smoke disappears and a giant gold genie appears*) I am a genie!
RYAN:	A ... a genie? You mean like a genie of the ... teapot?
GENIE:	Yes, Master.

1 **a** Ryan, Pritesh and a genie
  b in modern times
  c at a car boot sale
3 Ryan buys a teapot and his wishes start coming true.
4 A genie comes out of the teapot.
6-7 Answers will vary.

Unit 21

Page 46

5 a

I Wish

Ryan and Pritesh visit Nan at her home.
"Now then, what do we have here?" Nan asked.
"It's a present," Ryan said. "I hope you like it."
He gave Nan the teapot.
"Oh Ryan, it's lovely," Nan said, holding up the pot.
Ryan gave Pritesh a look that said, "I told you so."
"You are good boys," Nan said. "You know what I wish?"
"What's that, Nan?" said Ryan, watching the teapot.
"I wish I could win that lottery so I could really treat you both."
Just then there was a ring at the doorbell.
"Now who's that?" Nan said.
Ryan looked at Pritesh.
"Mrs Walker?" they heard a man say. "I have some very good news for you."

1 Answers will vary. Example: A Lucky Wish
2 Ryan, Pritesh, Ryan's grandmother (Nan, Mrs Walker), a man
3 Ryan's grandmother's (Nan's) house.
4 Answers may vary. Examples: *(Ryan and Pritesh are visiting Nan at her house.), (Ryan gives Nan the teapot.), (Nan holds up the pot.), (The doorbell rings.), (Nan answers the door.)*
5 **b** Answers will vary. Example:
  RYAN: It's a present, Nan. I hope you like it.
  RYAN: What's that Nan?

Unit 22

Page 49

1–5

Minecraft

Minecraft is one of the most popular video games of all time. It is both fun and educational. It is easy to learn and suitable for players over 8 years. It can be played on computers, game consoles, phones, tablets and even some televisions.

There is no story in Minecraft. Players build their own worlds using 3D blocks. While it may look simple at first, it becomes more complex as players progress. They use problem-solving skills and creativity to design and make their scenes. They can make anything from single buildings to farms, villages, cities and entire worlds. The only limit is their imagination. Players can choose between survival mode and creative mode. In survival mode, they have to build shelter and find food to stay healthy. They may even meet monsters to battle, but the monsters aren't scary. In creative mode, players can create whatever they want. There are no monsters in creative mode.

Minecraft is a fun game for anyone who likes to develop their thinking skills. Some say it can even help you become smarter.

6 Answers will vary. Example: I think you get even smarter when you play Minecraft.
7 most popular ... of all time, fun, educational, easy to learn, suitable for players over 8, make anything, only limit is their imagination, monsters aren't scary, create whatever they want, smarter

ANSWERS

Unit 24

Page 52

1 a Hannah and Josh
b at a bus stop
c one morning before school

2 a Hannah is at the bus stop when Josh arrives.
b Josh shoves a plastic spider at Hannah. Hannah screams.
c Josh calls Hannah a lung horn.
d The bus arrives. Hannah teases Josh about a snake.

3 Josh is frightened of the snake and rushes to get on the bus.

Term 3 Review

Page 54

1 a Josh raced to the school bus because there was a snake on the ground.
b The telescope won't work if the glasses are not at the right distance.
c There is no solar eclipse unless the Moon is between the Sun and the Earth.
d The children can't play Minecraft until they finish their homework.
e Whenever it rained a lot, the oval was always wet and slippery.

2 Answers will vary. Examples:
a The children couldn't watch TV until they finished their homework.
b The toaster won't work unless it's plugged in.
c The ground is always muddy because it always rains.
d You must keep the button pressed because it is faulty.
e You may see a shooting star if you look out at the sky tonight.
f The accountant takes her laptop home whenever she has weekend work.

3a **Make a Balloon Rocket**

Blow up a balloon and see it rocket across the room.

What you do

1 Tie one end of the string to a chair.
2 Thread the other end of the string through a straw.
3 Tie the string to another chair and pull it tight.
4 Blow up the balloon and pinch it, but don't tie it, so the air doesn't escape.
5 Tape the balloon to the straw.
6 Let the balloon go. Watch it fly across the room from one chair to the other.

3b • a balloon • two chairs
• some string • a straw

Page 55

4 Answers may vary. Example:

The Talking Dog

Characters: a man, a dog, a waiter

SCENE 1 *(in a restaurant)*

(A man and a dog enter a restaurant.)

WAITER: Sorry, sir. I will have to ask you to leave. Dogs aren't allowed in this restaurant.
MAN: But my dog is a talking dog. Won't you let us stay?
WAITER: *(looking surprised)* If your dog can talk, I will give you both a free meal!
MAN: *(to the dog)* What is above us in this restaurant?
DOG: Rrroof!
WAITER: *(to the dog)* Who is the greatest cricketer who ever lived?
DOG: Rrroof!
WAITER: You can't fool me. Your dog can't talk. You must leave immediately!

(The man and dog leave the restaurant.)

DOG: *(outside the restaurant)* Would it have made a difference if I'd said Donald Bradman?

5 Answers will vary.

TERM FOUR

Unit 25

Page 56

1 a The teacher, who is standing over there, is also the soccer coach.
b I bought my telescope at the shop that is on the corner.
c I gave my teapot to my grandmother whom you met yesterday.
d The movie, which we watched last night, was very funny.
e This plumber, whose quote was the cheapest, got the job.

2 Answers will vary. Examples:
a The elephant, that is in the enclosure by herself, has a new baby calf.
b The athlete, who is standing on the podium, won a gold medal.
c I returned the book to the library that is in the city.
d We bought a new video game at the video store which is just around the corner.

Page 57

3 a Although we had it fixed, the toaster still didn't work.
b The genie came out of the teapot whenever Ryan made a wish.
c The pianist practised every day so she would get better and better.

4 a Although we had it fixed, the toaster that we bought yesterday still didn't work.
b The genie who was as big as a giant, came out of the teapot whenever Ryan made a wish.
c The telescopes, which we made in class, were great because we could see the moon through them.

5 [Convicts who were sent to Australia were expected to work hard.] [When they first arrived, they had to bring supplies with them.] [By the early 1800s, a lot of the food that the settlers ate was grown in Australia.] [If the convicts were badly behaved, they could be punished.] [If they continued to misbehave, they could be sent to a penal colony such Norfolk Island or Port Arthur.] [If they behaved well, prisoners who were sentenced to seven years transportation were granted a Ticket of Leave, which allowed them to work for themselves.]

Unit 26

Page 59

1–3, 5–7

Bungaree

Bungaree, a Kuringgai man from the Broken Bay area in New South Wales, was the first Australian to circumnavigate Australia. He was born in about 1775 and moved to Sydney in the 1790s. He learned to speak English quickly and became well-known and liked in the area.

From 1801 to 1803, Bungaree sailed around Australia with Matthew Flinders, a British explorer. This was the first time anyone had sailed all around Australia. It proved that Australia was an island. It also made Bungaree the first Australian-born person to circumnavigate Australia. Bungaree helped keep the explorers safe. Although he didn't speak the same languages as the Indigenous Australian peoples who lived where they went ashore, Bungaree could communicate with them. He could also tell the explorers what plants were safe to eat and which to avoid.

Bungaree went on many other expeditions that explored Australia. He was the first Indigenous Australian person to receive a grant of land from the Governor. He died in Sydney in 1830 and is buried at Rose Bay.

3 a 1775 (about) born
  b 1790s moved to Sydney
  c 1801 to 1803 sailed around Australia
  d many other expeditions exploring Australia
  e first Indigenous Australian person to receive a grant of land
  f 1830 died
4 a Bungaree was the first Australian to circumnavigate Australia.
  b Bungaree was the first Indigenous Australian person to receive a grant of land from the Governor.

Unit 28

Page 62

1 Answers will vary. Examples:
  a Stars Shine Brightly
  b Umbrella Plays on a Sunny Day

2 a-c, 3 a, 4

Stars

[Stars shine brightly out their light,]
[Twinkling in the frosty night,]
[Hanging there for all to see,]
[And to wonder what they be,]
[Dotted on the dark backdrop,]
[Spattered paint on Earth's big top.]

Umbrella

[When white clouds dance across the sky,]
[You keep me where I'm safe and dry.]
[But when the dark clouds gather round]
[Making their obnoxious sound,]
[You take me out and hold me high,]
[So I get wet, and you stay dry.]
[And when the storm clouds roll away,]
[You shake me out, put me away,]
[I really wish you'd let me stay]
[And play with you on a sunny day.]

2 d Stars shine brightly out their light,
  Twinkling in the frosty night,
  e I really wish you'd let me stay
  And play with you on a sunny day.
3 b **Stars:** light/night, see/be, backdrop/big top
  Umbrella: sky/dry, round/sound, high/dry, away/away, stay/day
5 a Answers will vary. Examples:
  sparkling sky diamonds, glitter sprinkled on a black cat's back
  b Answers will vary. Example:
  enormous rainbow mushroom, protector from the rain

Unit 30

Page 67

1–3 a, 4, 5

Should Voting be Compulsory?

Frankie: Voting should be compulsory. It is a responsibility of everyone in a democratic society.
Alex: Surely people living in a democracy should be able to choose.
Frankie: People still have choices. They can leave the ballot paper blank or spoil it in some way. Or pay the $20 fine. When voting is compulsory, the winner really does win most votes and the support of most people. That doesn't happen when voting is voluntary.
Alex: But some might just vote for anyone, especially someone with an expensive ad campaign. And voting for someone you don't even like, just because you have to, doesn't make sense.
Frankie: People will be better informed and make better choices if they have to vote. Candidates will have to think about everyone in their electorate, not just the wealthy or vocal ones.
Alex: Even when voting is voluntary, people can still make their voices heard. Whether compulsory or not candidates should do a lot more to benefit those voting for them.

3 b Frankie: voting is the responsibility of everyone, the winner really does win, people will be better informed
  Alex: people should be able to choose, some might just vote for anyone, people can still make their voices heard
7 should, responsibility, really does, might just, don't even like, doesn't make sense, better informed, better choices, everyone
8 Answers will vary. Examples: definitely, must, important, essential, crucial

Unit 32

Page 70

1 We have lived in Lowtown for a long time. For all those years, we have never had a good reliable ambulance service. It is about time we did. Many people need access to medical treatment and are not getting it. Sometimes the ambulances take hours to come. Sometimes they come too late, and sometimes they don't come at all. It is just not good enough.
For years, the government has ignored our community. You must change this. We want to have our voices heard and our needs met. We pay taxes too. We need good medical care, just like everybody else. A reliable 24-hour ambulance service is part of that care. What will you do to make sure a reliable ambulance service is built in Lowtown? If you can't do this, then you are not representing all the people of your district.

2-4 Answers will vary.

Term 4 Review

Page 72

1 a Although he didn't speak the same languages as the Indigenous Australian peoples who lived where they went ashore, Bungaree could communicate with them.
  b Poems do not usually have sentences that follow the normal structure.
  c Each line of a stanza begins with a capital letter whether it is a new sentence or not.
  d Write a discussion that takes place when you are interviewed by someone who doesn't agree with your views.
  e It is important to eat nutritious food that is available everywhere so you stay healthy.
  f My mother, who is a doctor, had to work on the weekend because a lot of other doctors were sick with Covid.
  g Synthetic materials, which are made by people, are used to make many different products.
  h Astronauts, who live on the International Space Station, have to zip themselves into sleeping bags so they don't float out of the bags when they are asleep.

2 Answers will vary.

Page 73

3 & 4 Answers will vary.

Targeting Writing Skills Year 5

ISBN: 9781925726282
Published by Pascal Press
PO Box 250
Glebe NSW 2037
www.pascalpress.com.au
contact@pascalpress.com.au
Design: Janice Bowles
Author: Norah Colvin
Publisher: Lynn Dickinson
Editor: Marie Theodore
Typesetter: Stacey Grainger
Illustrator: Paul Lennon

Printed by Wai Man Book Binding (China) Ltd.